DIVIDE PAKISTAN

DIVIDE PAKISTAN

◆

TO ELIMINATE TERRORISM

Syed Jamaluddin

iUniverse, Inc.
New York Lincoln Shanghai

DIVIDE PAKISTAN
TO ELIMINATE TERRORISM

iUniverse books may be ordered through booksellers or by contacting:

iUniverse
2021 Pine Lake Road, Suite 100
Lincoln, NE 68512
www.iuniverse.com
1-800-Authors (1-800-288-4677)

ISBN-13: 978-0-595-41766-7 (pbk)
ISBN-13: 978-0-595-67934-8 (cloth)
ISBN-13: 978-0-595-86108-8 (ebk)
ISBN-10: 0-595-41766-3 (pbk)
ISBN-10: 0-595-67934-X (cloth)
ISBN-10: 0-595-86108-3 (ebk)

Printed in the United States of America

This Book is dedicated to

Khan Abdul Ghaffar Khan
(Bacha Khan)

Dr. G.M. Syed

Nawab Akbar Bugti

Contents

FOREWORD

In the words of Mr. Michael Evanoff (former Security Incharge at US Embassy in Pakistan):

'*This (Pakistan) is now the epicenter of terrorism. It really is. This is the only country I know in the world that has so many groups that are against the US or Western ideals.*'

He is right and very correct in his observation about Pakistan. Similarly, US President had said on September 20, 2001 in a policy statement that

"*Every nation in every region now has a decision to make. Either you are with us, or you are with the terrorists.*"

Implicitly, as long as Washington believed in the worth of Pakistan for US war against international terrorism, remote is the chance that Washington would still admit the demand to designate Pakistan as a terrorist state. In the war against terrorism, US remains unclear to most of peace-loving nations as how US perceives Pakistan's role as a state towards reigning in terrorism. US efforts, to soften the delicate balance of its individual bilateral relations with India and Pakistan, considerably lack effective communication in its response towards Indian grievance over cross border terrorism. Why does US not show determination to deal with Pakistan as a "terrorist state"? Apart from the US foreign policy in the post 9-11 world toward South Asia, such policy mainly revolves around three aspects viz US relationship with General Pervez Musharraf (despite acknowledging Pakistan as the hub of international terrorism), US shying away to take harder steps in dealing with General Pervez Musharraf and conceivable US political strategy against Iran involving Pakistan in the region.

Pakistan is basically a wolf in sheep's clothing. The National Commission on Terrorist Attacks Upon the United States (also known as the 9-11 Commission) cited evidence of Islamabad's collaboration with the Taliban before the terrorist attacks.

While Pakistan has made significant contributions to the war against terrorism, arresting a number of high-value al-Qaeda operatives, as claimed by Pakistan, yet the 9-11 Commission's report said that "the Taliban's ability to provide bin Laden a haven in the face of international pressure and UN sanctions was significantly facilitated by Pakistani support. According to another report from the *Congressional Research Service*, Pakistan has turned a blind eye to the Taliban and other militants who use its porous border regions as a launching pad for attacks against U.S., NATO and Afghani troops. The report, *Afghanistan: Post War Governance, Security and U.S. Policy* notes that "U.S. and Afghan officials continue to accuse Pakistan of allowing Taliban fighters to meet and group in Pakistani cities. An anonymous Western diplomat, quoted in the *New York Times*, was more colorful, saying "if you talk about the Taliban, its like fish in a barrel in Pakistan. They train, they rest there. They get support.

Ever since I was constrained to leave Pakistan as a result of undue pressure from Inter-Services Intelligence (ISI), a Pakistan-army sponsored intelligence agency engaged in terrorist activities around the world and its puppet religious cult group commonly known as Tablighi Jamat, based in Pakistan, when I had first revealed the truth behind the closed doors of Tablighi Jamat about their involvement in spreading hatred (among its followers and members) against Christians, Jews, Hindus and other Non-Muslim communities in the world on the basis of self-interpreted verses of Quran, I have never stopped writing the truth about Pakistan and its reality as a Terrorist State. My petition titled DIVIDE PAKISTAN TO ELIMINATE TERRORISM was first posted on www. petitiononline.com and www.voiceofthebelievers.com and thereafter several websites displayed the said petition. Certain newspapers also published this petition in 2001. My crusade against existence of Pakistan shall continue until I am able to convince the entire world community that Pakistan is a country of violence and terrorism. Pakistan is a curse. Pakistan is evil. Pakistan is neither an Islamic state nor a secular state. Pakistan is Terrorists' 'Dressing Room'.

Similarly, in my opinion, the term 'War-on-Terror' should exactly mean and be defined as a battle or crusade or say holy war against Tablighi Jamat and Inter-Services Intelligence (ISI) of Pakistan who are the producers/manufacturers of Taliban. These two dangerous groups have consistently facilitated empowerment of terrorists on this earth, in the name of *Jihad* through their well-organized and well-planned long term schemes, for destruction of Christians, Jews and Hindus wherever they live.

This book focuses attention towards the consequences which this world may face if Pakistan is further allowed to exist on the globe. Pakistan is not what it pretends to be. Pakistan has no justification to establish its legitimacy as a nation to be represented at the United Nations. Pakistan does not believe in allowing people of other religions to exist or live peacefully. When I say 'Pakistan', I always mean the vicious Pakistan Army and its puppet intelligence agency ISI along with its religious cult called Tablighi Jamat. Hence, in my opinion, 'Pakistan' does not and should not include peace-lovers like Pakhtoons, Sindhis, Baluchis, Kashmiris and those innocent Punjabis who are oppressed and marginalized by deadly Punjab's military dictatorship in Pakistan. Pakistan should, therefore, be disintegrated immediately.

Another reason to disintegrate Pakistan is the growing insecurity of small provinces of Pakistan. There is enough evidence on ground to call for a Plebiscite within these provinces of Pakistan to determine if people of these provinces really wish to live under the umbrella of Pakistan or not. As per the definition of ENCYCLOPEDIA BRITTANICA, Plebiscite means 'Vote by the people of an entire country or district to decide an issue. Voters are asked to accept or reject a given proposal rather than choose between alternative proposals. By means of plebiscites, intermediaries such as political parties can be bypassed. Because plebiscites offer a way to claim a popular mandate without permitting an opposition party, totalitarian regimes have used them to legitimize their power.' In view of this definition, people of Pakistan deserves a National Plebiscite. Hence, this book also advocates the need for an impartial PLEBISCITE in Pakistan whereby people from all 4 provinces (PUNJAB, NORTH WEST FRONTIER PROVINCE-NWFP, SINDH and BALUCHISTAN) and also 13 Million Urdu-speaking residents of Karachi and other nearby cities where Urdu-speaking people are in majority, should be allowed to decide if they wanted a United Pakistan or Divided Pakistan. I can guarantee that NWFP, Sindh and Baluchistan will always decide against United Pakistan and shall accordingly opt for their own respective new identities in the form of PAKHTOONISTAN, SINDHUDESH, BALUCHISTAN and JINNAHPUR (independent states). Such Plebiscite should be organized under the supervision of United Nations as immediately as possible after a specific resolution to be passed by Security Council of the United Nations.

My appeal to the whole world through this book is to bring Pakistan to justice by way of Plebiscite under supervision and monitoring of United Nations. This Plebiscite shall serve as an Acid-Test to prove the reality of Pakistan as a country. There is no political significance of Pakistan. Pakistan is nothing but simply a regime ruled by a few Punjabi military dictators and Inter-Services Intelligence (ISI). These rulers are a threat to international community since long. Time has come that comity of nations should realize the viciousness of Pakistan's existence in its present form. Disintegration of Pakistan was never essential than now in view of the dangers emanating from the soil of Pakistan.

I also request the readers of this book to understand the concept of Doctrine of Necessity as discussed in a separate chapter which highlights the need for invoking Doctrine of Necessity for dividing Pakistan in 5 parts in order to facilitate a genuinely balanced political strength in South Asia in particular and a peaceful political environment in the whole world in general. The best gift, which Mr. Bush and Mr. Blair can give to the whole world before they leave their offices, is disintegration of Pakistan which in turn means disintegration of real terrorist network. Please divide Pakistan to eliminate terrorism from the whole world.

Syed Jamaluddin
Aubervilliers
France
Jamal_ics@yahoo.com
September 26, 2006

MODERN FASCISM VS ISLAMIC FASCISM

Someone has said 'Fascism is a religious conception in which man is seen in his imminent relationship with a superior law and with an objective Will that transcends the particular individual and raises him to conscious membership of a spiritual society. Whoever has seen in the religious politics of the Fascist regime nothing but mere opportunism has not understood that Fascism besides being a system of government is also, and above all, a system of thought.'

The Fascist State, the highest and most powerful form of personality, is a force, but a spiritual force, which takes over all the forms of the moral and intellectual life of man. It cannot therefore confine itself simply to the functions of order and supervision as Liberalism desired. It is not simply a mechanism which limits the sphere of the supposed liberties of the individual. It is the form, the inner standard and the discipline of the whole person; it saturates the will as well as the intelligence. Its principle, the central inspiration of the human personality living in the civil community, pierces into the depths and makes its home in the heart of the man of action as well as of the thinker, of the artist as well as of the scientist: it is the soul of the soul.

Fascism, in short, is not only the giver of laws and the founder of institutions, but the educator and promoter of spiritual life. It wants to remake, not the forms of human life, but its content, man, character, faith. And to this end it requires discipline and authority that can enter into the spirits of men and there govern unopposed.

In the words of *Benito Mussolini:*

"Fascism, which was not afraid to call itself reactionary...does not hesitate to call itself illiberal and anti-liberal."

We all know the Nazis very well but our image is usually a caricature of a brutal soldier wearing a uniform emblazoned with a swastika. Most people in the U.S. are aware that the U.S. and its allies fought a war against the Nazis, but this is not enough for the new generation to just rely on, rather, they need to learn the important lessons of our recent history.

Technically, the word NAZI was the acronym for the 'National Socialist German Worker's Party'. It was a fascist movement that had its roots in the European nationalist and socialist movements. The seeds of Modern Fascism, however, were planted in Italy. "Fascism is reaction," said Mussolini, but reaction to what? The reactionary movement following World War I was based on a rejection of the social theories that formed the basis of the 1789 French Revolution, and whose early formulations in this country had a major influence on Declaration of Independence, Constitution, and Bill of Rights. Fascists particularly loathed the social theories of the French Revolution and its slogan: "Liberty, Equality, Fraternity."

*** Liberty from oppressive government intervention in the daily lives of its citizens, from illicit searches and seizures, from enforced religious values, from intimidation and arrest for dissenters; and liberty to cast a vote in a system in which the majority ruled but the minority retained certain inalienable rights.

*** Equality in the sense of civic equality, egalitarianism, the notion that while people differ, they all should stand equal in the eyes of the law.

*** Fraternity in the sense of the brotherhood of mankind. That all women and men, the old and the young, the infirm and the healthy, the rich and the poor, share a spark of humanity that must be cherished on a level above that of the law, and that binds us all together in a manner that continuously re-affirms and celebrates life.

This is what modern fascism as an ideology was reacting against and its support came primarily from desperate people anxious and angry over their perception that their social and economic position was sinking and frustrated with the constant risk of chaos, uncertainty and inefficiency implicit in a modern democracy based on these principles. Fascism is the antithesis of democracy. Western nations fought a war against it more than half a century ago; millions perished as victims of fascism and champions of liberty. In the words of *George Seldes* (Hartland Four Corners), Vermont, March 5, 1988:

"One of the great lies of this century is that in the 1930's General Franco in Spain was primarily a nationalist engaged in stopping the Reds. Franco was, of course, a fascist who was aided by Mussolini and Hitler."

"The history of this period is a press forgery. Falsified news manipulates public opinion. Democracy needs facts.

Modern Fascism was forged in the crucible of post-World War I nationalism in Europe. The humiliation imposed by the victors in the Great War, coupled with the hardship of the economic depression, created bitterness and anger. That anger frequently found its outlet in an ideology that asserted not just the importance of the nation, but its unquestionable primacy and central predestined role in history.

In Europe, Jews were the handy group to scapegoat as "them." Anti—Jewish conspiracy theories and discrimination against Jews were not a new phenomenon, but most academic studies of the period note an increased anti-Jewish fervor in Europe, especially in the late 1800's. In France this anti-Jewish bias was most publicly expressed in the case of Alfred Dreyfus, a French military officer of Jewish background, who in 1894 was falsely accused of treason, convicted (through the use of forged papers as evidence) and imprisoned on Devil's Island. Zola led a noble struggle which freed Dreyfus and exposed the role of anti-Jewish bigotry in shaping French society and betraying the principles on which France was building its democracy.

Italy was the birthplace of modern fascist ideology. Mussolini, a former socialist journalist, organized the first fascist movement in 1919 at Milan. In 1922 Mussolini led a march on Rome, was given a government post by the king, and began transforming the Italian political system into a fascist state. In 1938 he forced the last vestige of democracy, the Council of Deputies, to vote themselves out of existence, leaving Mussolini dictator of fascist Italy. Yet there were Italian fascists who resisted scapegoating and dehumanization even during World War II.

Franco's fascist movement in Spain claimed state power in 1936, although it took three years, the assistance of the Italian fascists and help from the secretly reconstituted German Air Force finally to crush those who fought for democracy. Picasso's famous painting depicts the carnage wrought in a Spanish village by the bombs dropped by the forerunner of the which all too soon would be working on an even larger canvas. Yet Franco's fascist Spain never adopted the obsession with race and anti-Jewish conspiracy theories that were hallmarks of Hitler's Nazi movement in Germany.

Other movements of modern fascism in Europe were more explicitly racialist, promoting the slogan still used today by some neo-Nazi movements: "Nation is Race." The Nazi racialist version of fascism was developed by Adolph Hitler who with six others formed the Nazi party during 1919 and 1920. Hitler was named Chancellor of Germany by Hindenburg in January 1933 and by year's end had consolidated his power as a fascist dictator and begun a campaign for racialist nationalism that eventually led to the Holocaust.

In the words of *Wilhelm Reich:*

"Reactionary concepts plus revolutionary emotion result in Fascist mentality."

One element shared by all fascist movements, racialist or not, is the apparent lack of consistent political principle behind the ideology and political opportunism in the most basic sense. One aspect of modern fascism is its ruthless drive to attain and hold state power. On that road to power, fascists are willing to abandon any principle to adopt an issue more in vogue and more likely to gain converts. Hitler, for his part, committed his act of abandonment bloodily and dramatically. When the industrialist power brokers offered control of Germany to Hitler, they knew he was supported by national socialist ideologues who held views incompatible with their idea of profitable enterprise. What distinguishes Nazism from modern fascism is its obsession with racial theories of superiority.

Modern Fascism involves, to varying degrees, some of the following hallmarks:

*** Nationalism and super-patriotism with a sense of historic mission.

*** Aggressive militarism even to the extent of glorifying war as good for the national or individual spirit.

*** Use of violence or threats of violence to impose views on others (fascism and Nazism both employed street violence and state violence at different moments in their development).

*** Authoritarian reliance on a leader or elite not constitutionally responsible to an electorate.

*** Cult of personality around a charismatic leader.

*** Reaction against the values of Modernism, usually with emotional attacks against both liberalism and communism.

*** Exhortations for the homogeneous masses of common folk to join voluntarily in a heroic mission often metaphysical and romanticized in character.

*** Dehumanization and scapegoating of the enemy seeing the enemy as an inferior or subhuman force, perhaps involved in a conspiracy that justifies eradicating them.

*** The self image of being a superior form of social organization beyond socialism, capitalism and democracy.

*** Elements of national socialist ideological roots, for example, ostensible support for the industrial working class or farmers; but ultimately, the forging of an alliance with an elite sector of society.

*** Abandonment of any consistent ideology in a drive for state power.

It is vitally important to understand that modern fascism or Nazism are not biologically or culturally determinant. Modern Fascism does not attach to the gene structure of any specific group or nationality. Nazism was not the ultimate expression of the German people. The origin of Modern Fascism did not end with World War II.

In the words of Hitler: "The great masses of people…will more easily fall victims to a big lie than to a small one."

In the light of above arguments, I would like to draw the attention of readers to the fact the modern fascism is basically replication of Islamic fascism which was born about 1500 years ago on the death of Islam's holy prophet Muhammad. If we examine the post-Muhammad era of Islam, it is the beginning of Islamic fascism whereby the people who took charge of Islam were, in the light of above definitions and arguments, undoubtedly Islamic Fascists. The first three caliphs of Islam viz Abu Bakr, Omar bin Khattab and Usman bin Affan laid the foundation of an Islamic Fascism which consolidated their mutual efforts to hijack a religion which was later popularly spread from the soil of Mecca in a manner favourable to such Fascists and not in accordance with the sayings of Muhammad or his genuine follower i.e. Ali, his son-in-law.

These first three Caliphs of Islam introduced the various theories of dictatorship which were later idealized by all such forces, in different parts of this world, who were interested in persecution of humanity and development of an architecture of fear. In my opinion, the first three Caliphs of Islam were 'Architects of Fear' among people. This fear caused disintegration among the followers of Muhammad so much so that history of Islam is full of bloodshed and violence due to such conflicting beliefs and attitudes. Modern Fascism could not be born without a *father*. And *father* of modern fascism is Islam itself.

Modern Fascism gave birth to the following dictators:

- Sani Abacha in Nigeria

- Field Marshal Ayub Khan in Pakistan

- General Yahya Khan in Pakistan

- General Zia-ul-Haq in Pakistan

- General Pervez Musharraf in Pakistan

- Moammar Qaddafi in LIbya

- Idi Amin in Uganda

- Jean-Bedel Bokassa in the Central African Republic

- Francisco Franco in Spain

- Adolf Hitler in Germany

- Saddam Hussain in Iraq

- Benito Mussolini in Italy

- Robert Mugabe in Zimbabwe

- Manuel Noriega in Panama

- Augusto Pinochet in Chile

- Raza Shah Pahelvi of Iran

- Charles Taylor in Liberia

- Tito in Yugoslavia

Symbols of Islamic Fascism

Abu Bakr, Omar bin Khatab, Usman Ibn Affan, Mawiya and Yazeed were the founders of Islamic Fascism.

Abu Bakr

Abu Bakr was the first Caliph of Islam after death of Muhammad SA. In my opinion, first of all, Abu Bakr should not be viewed as a genuine companion of Muhammad SA. The Wahabi Islam sponsored by Saudi Kingdom (as discussed in detail in other chapter of this book) has propagated the superior status of Abu Bakr due to one certain event whereby Abu Bakr had hidden inside the cave with Muhammad SA while escaping to Medina from Mecca due to severe persecution by infidels of Mecca. This act of Abu Bakr of hiding with Muhammad SA cannot be considered as a brave act. The argument is very simple which can be under-stood even by any primary level pupil of the 21st century that such hiding by Abu Bakr did not constitute a merit in itself, as any merit should be derived from his action and behavior there. Abu Bakr himself confessed the truth in the following words:

Narrated Abu Bakr: I was with the Prophet in the Cave. When I raised my head, I saw the feet of the people. I said, "O Allah's Apostle! If some of them should look down, they will see us." The Prophet said, "O Abu Bakr, be quiet! (For we are) two and Allah is the Third of us." (Sahi Bukhari 58.259)

If this answer of Muhammad SA is presented in front of present day jury of any competent judicial system, the statement of Muhammad SA "O Abu Bakr, be quiet!" cannot be considered as a 'tribute' or 'praise'. It rather shows how Muhammad SA had scolded Abu Bakr who was getting nervous, excited and fearful at that time because he was a coward. Similarly, the fact that Abu Bakr was referred to as the "Companion" (Sahib) of the Prophet in the Cave, as in the Qur'an, does not show any dignity or upper status of Abu Bakr for the simple reason that in the same Quran, Yousuf AS (named Joseph in Bible) who had talked to two **disbelievers** in prison, these disbelievers were also referred to as his "Companions" because they were in close physical proximity to him, clearly showing that the word "Companion" in the Qur'an is not necessarily attributing any special significance to Abu Bakr. Hence, the using of term 'Companion' for

Abu Bakr does not represent a high status, but just may describe the physical proximity of someone to another person.

It is also very amusing to note that the Wahabi Islam sponsored and supported by the Saudi Kingdom portrays Abu Bakr as a super star or celebrity of that time. However, it is found in the books of Islamic history that when Abu Bakr had returned to Medina after the news of Muhammad's (SA) death reached him, at that point, another colleague of Abu Bakr having similar characteristics like him known as Omar bin Khattab began threatening people to be killed if they spread the news of Muhammad's (SA) death. While Abu Bakr was in the house where Muhammad's (SA) body was kept, accompanied with the rest of Banu Hashim, the said Omar bin Khattab informed Abu Bakr of the meeting of Saqifah. I personally believe that Abu Bakr leaving the house without informing anyone of the meeting, proves that he went there in bad faith with mala fide intent. This was indeed beginning of a possible dictatorship to surface...an era of Islamic fascism to kick off.

The hypocrisy of Abu Bakr can also be justified from the very fact that he entered into a dispute with Muhammad's only then living child Bibi Fatima AS so much so that the beloved daughter of Muhammad SA refused to talk with Abu Bakr for the rest of her life (almost six months). Hence, it is proved that Abu Bakr had no respect of Muhammad SA at all as Wahabi scholars always paint the picture of Abu Bakr. Dont forget that it is always habit of a dictator to dominate his own plans and invoke his own strategy in dealing with matters of State. So did Abu Bakr who despite having been involved in tremendous victories along with Muhammad SA during the lifetime of Muhammad SA, still proved his hypocritic approach soon after the death of Muhammad SA. This was the reason that several Muslim tribes refused to pay Tax (Zakat) to Abu Bakr but they did not deny the need to pay Zakat, nor any other Muslim principle. Such refusal was in line with their firm belief that Abu Bakr was a dictator and a fascist. If we recall the military dictatorship of General Zia-ul-Haq who also represented the same man-made Wahabi Islam sponsored by Saudi Kingdom, the Shias in Pakistan refused to pay Tax (Zakat) to the Government on the same grounds. Hence, it can be well established that dictators have always existed. The only important thing is to identify them. Such identification can only take place if the people are on the right path. Another glaring evidence of Abu Bakr's fascism was his appointing of former dictator of Mecca known as Abu Sufyan who was Muhammad's SA former arch enemy. This arbitrary act of Abu Bakr has confirmed that Abu Bakr was an old member of Fascists' Club of Mecca, yet, he had embraced Islam after thoroughly understanding the future prospects of Islam like any other knowledgable person of that particular time. After all, Fascists are not fools. Hitler was not a fool either but he was indeed a fascist of his own kind. In my opinion, fascists are more intelligent and cunning than other people as they observe the chronology of events and view the circumstances more effectively and courageously. That is why, if I compare Abu Bakr with Hitler, there are certain similarities such as Hitler had appointed cruel Generals to persecute innocent jews while Abu Bakr also appointed Khalid ibn Walid as his right hand to handle army actions which killed several people, including several close companions of Muhammad SA during the first days of Islam. These killings included **Malik bin Nuwaira** who was a chief of the Bani Yarbu (a famous tribe composed of a large section of the powerful tribe of Bani Tamim which inhabited the north-eastern region of Arabia, above Bahrain). Khalid Ibn Walid "married" widow of Malik bin Nuwaira that same night. This was not marriage but a brutal rape committed by a person commonly referred as a most « pious » and « God-fearing » by Muslims belonging to Wahabi Islam sponsored by Saudi Kingdom. Is it not a mockery of facts that on one hand, Islam says that it is impossible to marry any divorcee woman or widow before the end of her three menses (almost 4 months), yet, the fascist associate of Abu Bakr committed such a brutal crime so openly under the nose of his boss Abu Bakr. Even Abu Bakr sided with Khalid bin Walid and protected him. I, therefore, view Abu Bakr as pioneer of Islamic fascism and view him as a persecutor of Muslims evidenced by his acts of employing the former arch-enemies of Islam as his highest generals, and protecting them when they committed murders and sexual assaults.

Omar bin Kattab

I do not keep Omar bin Khattab in high esteem and do not consider him as one of the best Companions of Muhammad. Rather, I hold an opposing perspective of him. I do not view him as a legitimate leader of the then Muslim nation and believe it to be factually provable that Omar bin Khattab and Abu Bakr (as discussed above) conspired to usurp power from Ali, who was the deserving son-in-law of Muhammad. In my opinion, Omar bin Khattab was another Fascist leader after the death of Abu Bakr and his socalled popularity created by Wahabi scholars of Saudi Kingdom as a just ruler is mainly a 'false work' conducted by Umayyad (term "Umayyad" is Greek, referring to "Banu Umayyah" (the Tribe of Umayyah) which refers to those who descended from Umayya Bin Abd Shams). I believe that the Umayyad view was propagated with lethal force and heavy duress and as time went on, that view became predominant and eventually taken as truth, cemented by the works of Bukhari (Wahabi source of hadith-collection comprised of sayings of Muhammad).

This is not a fact to be ignored that Omar was an idol worshiper and that this disqualifies him from being a leader for all Muslims. I persoanlly believe that no God-appointed Muslim leader has ever worshipped anything or anyone else otherthan God. In other words, a man designated to protect and guide all Muslims at least must have a pure enough character to have refrained from the grossest sin in Islam. It is purity of character which should be addressed on this issue and not sin, not to be confused with the removal of sin due to accepting Islam. Omar bin Khattab was also involved in an abusive act of burrying his own daughters. Omar had buried alive his own daughter, despite it being a characteristic of the time he lived in. Another point which makes Omar bin Khattab very low is about the low morale of his family, exemplified by his uncle, Omar ibn Nufayl, marrying his own mother. In other words, Omar had belonged to a family involved in incest. We cannot just ignore these facts about Omar bin Khattab simply because he had embraced Islam. I doubt the sincerity of Omar bin Khattab as a true Muslim and hence consider him as another Fascist leader in the disguise of a Muslim leader. The story how Omar bin Khattab embraced Islam is known to almost all Muslims, but, I could not understand the aggressive and arrogant character of Omar bin Khattab until I saw Sultan Rahi (a Punjabi Movie Star from Pakistan) in several movies in Punjabi language in which he had acted exactly how Omar bin Khattab acted in Mecca…shouting, challenging, alarming, provoking and yet very arrogant and aggressive at all times…ready to kill and slaughter.

The fascist character of Omar bin Khattab is very identical to other dictators like Hitler, Zia-ul-Haq, Mussolini, Saddam Hussain and now Pervez Musharraf. The Wahabi scholars have given undue respect to Omar's blunt, agitative, arrogant and deplorable character in order to exhibit his socalled 'devotion' and 'anger' for Islam. I do not believe that Omar's strength is to be applauded because he abused it repeatedly. For example, he beat people in a mosque and threatened Muslims in front of Muhammad. Omar beat Abu Huraira (a very renowned companion of Muhammad) severely on several occasions, both during Muhammad's life and after. Also, Omar publicly and loudly questioned Muhammad's authority at the Treaty of Hudaybia (the famous Hudaybia truce with infidels). After been given an answer and not being content with it, he went to Abu Bakr (his old fascist friend) and again questioned Muhammad's authority. I do not see Omar as a valiant man at all even though he was strong. In my personal opinion, Omar was a coward since there are scarce reports of Omar hurting anyone or even getting hurt in any battle. In fact, he was notorious for not entering combat. When the battle of Uhud went awry and rumors of Muhammad's death started, Omar fled the battle, ran to a hill and discouraged people from entering battle again, arguing that there was no point fighting since Muhammad was dead. In the famous Battle of Trench (the name "Battle of the Trench" comes from the fact that the Muslims dug a trench north of Medina to protect the city Medina since Medina was naturally fortified on all other fronts), Omar did not obey commandment of his superior officer. Also, at Khyber (It was inhabited by Jews long before the rise of Islam, and gave refuge to the Jewish Banu Nadir tribe), Omar did not direct his troops against the fortress.

Omar's father, al-Khattab, was a staunch follower of idolatry. I do not see or understand if Omar Khattab could be known as a true follower of Islam in the perspective enshrined by Quran since his blood was indeed mixed with an idolator. Even though Omar evidently was mistaken on several occasions, which is clearly seen by the evidence, he has still set precedence in Wahabi jurisprudence. Thus, there is an ample need to enlighten people of Omar's ignorance, so that they stop following a man that believed he could shape the 'lifestyle' of Muhamamd.

Even though Omar did make numerous 'religious decrees' in direct violation to the Quran, the Wahabi scholars have agreed to put Omar bin Khattab on top simply to exhibit and strengthen their hatred for Ali, son-in-law of Muhammad. I believe that Omar was the main fascist leader who acted as a force behind Abu Bakr's rise to power, since basically it was Omar bin Khattab who had stopped Abu Bakr from giving in to Fatima's (Muhammad's daughter) cries for justice after the death of Muhammad. Omar was also responsible for the election that followed after him, an election which was openly rigged to the extent that the deserving Ali (son-in-law of Muhammad) could not win it, hence, giving away the Muslim nation to Islam's former arch-enemies, the Banu Umayyad (children of Umayyad, starting with Usman and continuing with the adopted son of Abu Sufyan, Mawiya, followed by Yazeed, resulting in the slaughter of Hussain (grand son of Muhammad) in the famous battle of Karbala and ultimately the pillage and rape of Medina and the criminal assault on the Kaba (the house of God in Mecca). I have a firm belief that many hadith where Omar is merited by Muhammad are nothing more than late Umayyad fabrications. Omar was Mussolini of that time or vice versa.

Usman Ibn Affan

Like Abu Bakr and Omar bin Khattab, Usman Ibn Affan was a usurper and an enemy of Ali, the son-in-law of Muhammad. Usman Ibn Affan was guilty of nepotism, corruption, double-dealing, and turning the empire over to Muhammad's SA old enemies, the Umayyads. I firmly believe that Usman, like many of the other early Muslims, was seduced by the pleasures of power and wealth, and strayed from the strict path of Islam. In the words of Bernard Lewis:

"Usman, like Mawiya, was a member of the leading Meccan family of Ummaya and was indeed the sole representative of the Meccan patricians among the early companions of the Prophet with sufficient prestige to rank as a candidate. His election was at once their victory and their opportunity. That opportunity was not neglected. Usman soon fell under the influence of the dominant Meccan families and one after another of the high posts of the Empire went to members of those families. The weakness and nepotism of Usman brought to a head the resentment which had for some time been stirring obscurely among the Arab warriors. The Muslim tradition attribute the breakdown which occurred during his reign to the personal defects of Usman. But the causes lie far deeper and the guilt of Usman lay in his failure to recognize, control or remedy them."

Hence, Usman Ibn Affan was though member of the same club of fascists, yet, he was more famous in the area of corruption committed by his relatives and loved ones.

Mawiya

Mawiya is the most vicious fascist leader in the history of Islam (I mean Wahabi Islam sponsored by Saudi Kingdom). Mawiya ibn Abi-Sufyan was born in a powerful clan known as Banu Abd Shams of the Quraysh tribe. The Quraysh controlled the city of Mecca, in what is now western Saudi Arabia, and the Banu Abd-Shams were among the most influential of its citizens. Mawiya's father Abu Sufyan and mother Hind are famous hypocrites in their own right. Many of the Abd-Shams opposed Muhammad SA when he was preaching his new faith in Mecca, and joined in the armed battles that followed the flight of Muhammad and his followers to Medina. In 630 CE, Muhammad SA and his followers conquered Mecca, and most of the Meccans, including the Abd-Shams, formally submitted to Muhammad and accepted Islam. According to some historians, Mawiya embraced Islam in defiance of his relatives. But, in my personal opinion, Mawiya had not converted until after the conquest of Mecca. He was among the worshippers of rising sun. Muhammad SA welcomed his former opponents, enrolled them in his army and gave them important posts in the expanding Islamic empire. Mawiyah became one of Muhammad's SA scribes. After Muhammad's SA death in 632, he served in the Islamic army sent against the Byzantine forces in present-day Syria.

Maweya bin Hind is a character whose antics have been meticulously recorded in the annals of history. From his birth onwards, the historians have managed to provide a significant insight in to the character of Maweya. His role within the history if Islam during the advent of Prophet Muhammad's SA mission is non-existent. In fact he spent the vast portion of it on the opposite side with his alleged father being 'Abu Sufyan leader of the Banu Umayya Clan who sought to undermine, fight and destroy the message of the Muhammad SA. Abu Sufyan eventually conceded defeat following the conquest of Mecca and allegedly embraced Islam. In the same way as Muhammad SA was opposed by Abu Sufyan, his alleged son Maweya carried on the mantle of his father opposing Ali AS (son-in-law of Muhammad SA) during his lifetime, refusing to give him bayya (oath of allegiance) and even after his martyrdom vented his hatred of Ali AS via the disgraceful practice of cursing him during the Friday Sermons.

Mawiya's enmity towards Muhammad SA did not restrict him to just opposing Ali AS and other descendants of Muhammad SA, but also made him murder several companions and a wife of Muhammad as well.

He killed Ayesha RA (widow of Muhammad SA) in cold blood after ordering the killing of her brother Muhammad bin Abu Bakar. He was also responsible for the killings of many other companions of Muhammad SA including Hajar bin Adi and Ammar Yasir. Despite his disgraceful acts, Wahabis under the umbrella of Saudi Kingdom have appeared in recent years declaring their affiliation with Mawiya and defending his actions and praising them.

One source revealed the story of murder of Ayesha RA (widow of Muhammad SA) in following words:

"Mawiya invited Ayesha RA for dinner, and he got a ditch dug in the ground, filling it up with sharp knives and swords, with their blades facing upwards. According to Alama Ibn Khaldoon, Mawiya masked that ditch with lanky pieces of wood, and spread a carpet on top of it all to camouflage it. He placed a wooden chair over it for Ayesha to sit. No sooner Ayesha sat on the chair, the whole set up retrieved and she fell in the pit, injuring herself from head to toe, and breaking a lot of bones. To hide his felony, Mawiya got the ditched filled up with lime. That is how he murdered Ayesha RA. She was sixty four years old when Mawiya murdered her towards the end of 57 Hijri. This proves, with out a doubt, that Maweya was an enemy of Muhammad SA, and he proved his enmity towards Muhammad SA by murdering his beloved wife. The only reason that Mawiya performed this heinous act was that Ayesha stopped him from making fun of Islam from the pulpit of Masjid-e-Nabvi. This is why no one knows the exact location of Ayesha's grave in Medina."

Mawiya was a nefarious politician. He was the son of Abu Sufyan, the leader of Mecca, who spent his whole life opposing Mhammad SA in Mecca. He was also the leader of every pagan army that fought against the Islamic armies. Maweya's mother was Hinda, who had eaten body parts of Hamza (RA) who was Muhammad's SA uncle. Maweya never accepted Islam sincerely in his heart. After the conquest of Mecca by Muhammad SA, both Mawiya and his father Abu Sufyan accepted Islam as DOCTRINE OF NECESSITY with a loathing heart. After the murder of Usman bin Affan, Maweyah rebelled against the fourth elected caliph Ali RA. All Historians have mentioned in disgust that Maweya (the governor of Damascus) back stabbed Islam when he made a thirty year peace treaty with the Roman king, rather than fighting for Islam, according to which Syria came under the rule of Roman empire and Mawiya agreed to give thirty thousand coins, fifty Arab slaves and fifty Arab horses to the Roman king every year. This act of Mawiya is very similar to General Pervez Musharraf's present day romance with Americans whereby Musharraf is offering all possible assistance to Americans in the name of War-on-Terror to keep his illegitimate dictatorship well in place. All of the Muslims of that era had disliked this brutal act of Mawiya and cursed him, hence, people of Pakistan have also cursed these acts of gesture of General Pervez Musharraf. In my opinion, Musharraf of today is very similar to Mawiya of yester years. Both are fascists.

Yazeed bin Mawiya

Yazeed bin Mawiya was yet another cruel fascist known as a hero in Wahabi Islam. Yazeed bin Mawiya had killed Hussain AS, the grand son of Muhammad SA, in a battle in Karbala (Iraq) because Hussian AS had refused to accept Yazeed's rule as a King. Yazeed was not a Muslim like his father but this fact was known to very few people at that time including Hussain AS. Since, the religious scholars of Wahabi Islam (sponsored by Saudi Kingdom) consider Yazeed as a prince because he was son of Mawiya, this philosophy has been propagated by Tablighi Jamat since last 80 years. Today, Yazeed is cursed by true Muslims but loved by hypocrites of Wahabi Islam.

General Zia-ul-Haq

General Zia-ul-Haq was another fascist whose name shall remain alive in the history of dictators. His most vicious legacy was his fighting the Soviet-Afghan war by proxy, in an alliance with the Afghan resistance, created by Inter-Services Intelligence (ISI) the Mujahideen (Muslim Fighters), against the invading USSR. His open accepting of financial assistance from the USA to fight the Soviet Union displayed his fascist character very glaringly. He was then instrumental in providing military aid to the socalled Muslim Fighters fighting in Afghanistan against Soviet occupation and then later diverting them to the Kashmir cause in the late 1980s. His major sins included complete Soviet withdrawal by 1988, which perhaps stopped a direct military invasion of Pakistan which could have resulted in division of Pakistan in 5 parts for which now I am making my sincere efforts after so many years.

General Zia also militarized the bureaucracy systematically. By his government's orders, 5 % of all new posts in the higher civil service were to be filled by army officers who, consequently, occupied important civilian positions. This act of General Zia makes him very identical to Usman Ibn Affan who also had done the same thing. Usman Ibn Affan, being a dictator and fascist of his own style, had distributed important positions of his government among members of his own tribe.

General Zia's socalled Wahabiat policy also proved to be extremely influential, and has continued to affect the political and sectarian situation in Pakistan till the present day. The nation's liberal elements claim that the late General's policy gave rise to previously unknown sectarianism and religious fanaticism within the country. Here, General Zia looks very identical to Mawiya and Yazeed since these two cruel fascists also imposed their own brand of Islam on people. General Zia's Wahabiat policies restored a sense of bias against Ali, son-in-law of Muhammad SA and Hussain AS, grand son of Muhammad SA. These two noble personalities of true Islam are considered as enemies in Wahabi brand of Islam (sponsored by Saudi Kingdom) as propagated by Tablighi Jamat.

General Pervez Musharraf

General Pervez Musharraf is a symbolic replication of above-noted Fascists from the Islamic history. Shortly after the 1999 coup, General Musharraf told the nation: "I shall not allow the people to be taken back to the era of sham democracy." Four years later, the people realized that Musharraf has truly kept his word. He did not allow anyone to take people back to the era of sham democracy. He did it himself. The lesson General Musharraf and his Western backers are leaving behind for other coup leaders in this process is: If the constitution does not legitimize your actions, delegitimize the constitution. That you can do by virtue of holding it in abeyance. In the meanwhile, instead of mending your ways, amend the constitution to legitimize both your actions and the "sacred" document. The brutal murder of Akbar Bugti, the great Baluch freedom fighter is a glaring example of Musharaff's ability to follow the footsteps of his Muslim ancestors (Abu Bakr, Omar bin Khattab, Usman and Mawiya) whom he loves very much as a true Wahabi Muslim within the definition followed by Saudi Kingdom. It might sound odd and impossible but not for someone backed up by absolute power. The former sham Pakistani democracies now seem far better by comparison when looked at in the perspective of all the crusaders of democracy fully approving and supporting a people's living under a systematically legalized dictatorship exactly in the same manner as happened during the tenure of Abu Bakr, Omar bin Khattab and Mawiya. Those who still have doubts need only to begin with amendments to Pakistan's constitution that "legitimize all the actions and deeds of General Pervez Musharraf since he seized power in a military coup six years ago,"—and see what actions has it really endorsed. Omar bin Khattab changed certain laws of Islam and so Musharraf committed the same crime by changing the Constitution. Both have similar fascist approach.

I would like to know if there is any legitimacy on the part of Pakistan to remain in existence with such rulers who are as brutal as dangerous animals in jungle.

WHY DISINTEGRATE PAKISTAN?

Pakistan should immediately be disintegrated under the supervision of the United Nations because a mushroom cloud of Islamic militancy or commonly known as jihadi Islam is casting its grim shadow over Pakistan under the sponsorship of Inter-Services Intelligence (ISI). The fallout from it in the form of growing internal political tensions and international isolation is already being felt in Pakistan.

What is perhaps more sobering is the insidious potential it carries to break up the federal structure of Pakistan, regardless of the mythologies that have been maintained about the unifying bonds of federally sponsored Wahabi Islam propagated by certain religious groups (both political and non-political). Islamic Ideology was converted into Jihadi Islam during the Afghan war against Soviet Union. Similarly, there is a phenomenal continuity between the "Islamic Ideology," used interchangeably with "Ideology of socalled Pakistan". The Ideology of Pakistan, the construction of which began soon after independence, maintains that Pakistan's nationhood is founded exclusively on religion and belief in Islam is the only force which will keep Pakistan's federation together. This perception has now proved to be totally false since there has never been any credible evidence to support this unfounded idea or basis.

On the contrary, the most turbulent events in the history of Pakistan clearly point to the failure of so called Islamic Ideology to serve as a viable basis for national unity due to influence of one single province known as Punjab which dominated the entire country under the auspices of vicious military dictatorship. Consequently, mere Islamic bonds did not even prevent East Pakistan (as discussed above) from seceding in 1971 and national unity did not fair any better in the territorially diminished Pakistan.

Similarly, the Baloch alienation from the federation resulted in an insurrection that lasted from 1973 todate only to be suppressed by massive military operations

17

including the recent one on August 26, 2006 when Nawab Akbar Bugti (freedom fighter for Baluchistan) was brutally murdered by Pakistan Army in a socalled encounter. Even in the past, in 1983 when the Movement for Restoration of Democracy (MRD) issued a call for civil disobedience, the people of interior Sind responded with a spontaneous uprising against the federal authority which was again put down with a brutal and prolonged military crackdown.

Common faith in Islam had also failed to prevent the bloody ethnic and sectarian conflicts in Pakistan's most populated city called Karachi during 1992. Yet the diehard ideologists of Pakistan (who are none other than paid intellectuals of Punjab) have never refrained to wonder if there might be something seriously flawed in their convictions. They continue to insist that common faith in Islam is not only a necessity but sufficient condition for preserving the national unity of this socalled Pakistan and the integrity of its federal structure. They are not ready to accept that Pakistan is not a result of any prophecy of Holy Prophet of Islam.

If Pakistan has suffered dismemberment in the past and disaffection with the federation continues to mount, it only calls for a stronger reaffirmation of Pakistan's Islamic roots and vigorous state action to implement Islamic ideology in practice. The project of Islamization through state sponsorship also got under way with a great leap forward under the fascist dictatorship of Gen. Ziaul Haq (1977–1988). Without a popular mandate to govern, and driven by his compulsion to legitimize his rule, General Zia had moved forcibly and criminally to "WAHABIZE" the Pakistani state and society. On the one hand he issued a stream of martial law and presidential ordinances to introduce an "Islamic system" or Nizam-e-Islam" as it was called, and on the other hand he involved Pakistan in the holy war to take on the Soviet infidels in Afghanistan, to be rewarded by an immediate renewal of US military and economic aid which had been blocked for some time.

More significantly, as the reality of this process began to impinge upon the daily lives of women and men, all the questions and contradictions concealed in the past rhetoric of Islamic ideology began to surface sharply in view. Which type of Islam? Is it the one 'MADE IN SAUDI ARABIA' or 'MADE IN IRAN', or 'MADE IN INDONESIA' or 'MADE IN PAKISTAN BY ISI UNDER THE AUSPICES OF TABLIGHI JAMAT' or any other type? These and similar questions were now thrown open into the public arena. But given the state of Pakistan's civil society, cramped under authoritarian regimes, answers to these questions could not emerge as a result of public debate and consensus. Instead they became evidence of a failed state called Pakistan. The conflict has since widened to pave way for disintegration of Pakistan, yet, it is a strange conflict.

While the stakes are great for Pakistan and its people the Islamist parties most fiercely engaged in the combat happen to be culturally, spiritually and geographically alien to much of the country. This is a fact which has gone generally unnoticed, but cannot be escaped if a little closer attention is paid to the historical background of the Islamist parties, their involvement in Pakistan's politics and their doctrinal positions. We will find that all such religious groups are composed of hypocrites.

Time has come that no more time should be wasted by the international powers and particularly the United Nations to divide/disintegrate Pakistan as immediately as possible in order to block the terrorist networks currently nourished within the jurisdiction of this country. People in USA, Israel, UK, India and all over Europe & Asia know this glaring fact that Pakistan's involvement in sponsoring international terrorism is no more hidden from the eyes of international comity of nations. The role of this country is not only to provide all logistical support to the militants who are trained under supervision of its institutions like ISI but also to mobilize new forces to combat all efforts being made by the West in restoration of peace in Middle East.

Pakistan's role is indeed very suspicious as Pakistan disguises itself as an ally of USA in war-on-terror although its own army and intelligence agencies are busy day-&-night monitoring the ongoing situation in Middle East including Iraq, Lebanon and Palestine. Not only fresh student visas are being issued to terrorists in the name of their religious education in Pakistan but the Pak Government has decided recently to ensure that such 'students' be educated in the field of Computer Science and Journalism in order to make them 'useful' members of society. This is indeed alarming that all of a sudden, the religious schools of Pakistan have decided to come out of the 'stone-age' and adopt modern educational skills in order to become compatible to other fellow institutions in the country.

This revolutionary change is not at all caused due to any public demand or their anxiety to explore new ways of progessive educational system but simply to fight the West whom they call as « infidels ». The sole reason of this new advancement in the name of innovation and development is none other than making and improving plans to create more scientific and effective schemes of destruction of Christians, Jews and Hidus. Pakistan is therefore providing all possible strength and support for such acts of engineered terrorism from its soil. This fact is fully in knowledge of USA, UK and all other members of the UN Security Council, however, current international political situation does not allow them to say a word or make an attempt to spark this fire at this time. But, such a global reluctance does not mean that Pakistan should be ignored in such a way.

There has to be some way to solve this problem once and for all. The solution is to disintegrate Pakistan immediately under the UN's supervision in the best interest of international peace and mankind. Any further negligence may cause more destruction in nearest future. Pakistan is not only producing new army of terrorists but also strengthening their institutional network from its soil. ISI's direct link with Tablighi Jamat (Islamic Preaching Group) based in Raiwind (near Lahore-Pakistan) is no more a fabricated story. Presence and participation of ISI's officials in meetings held at headquarters of Tablighi Jamat simply show the exact picture of a well-designed, well-controlled and well-managed strategy to prepare and train combatants in the disguise of 'preachers' who will fight in the 'name of Allah' against the 'enemies of Islam'.

A purely Islamised brain-washing methodology is at work in almost 1,000,000 mosques around the country where Tablighi Jamat has already spread its network through local workers termed as 'Saathi' (Fellow Workers). These socalled companions are motivated to follow the guidelines and lessons of guidance given by their elders stationed at the headquarters of Tablighi Jamat in Raiwind-Lahore-Pakistan.

United Nations, United States of America and all members of the Security Council should understand the dangers of terrorism emanating from a United Pakistan under the military leadership of Punjab. Pakistan's military dictatorship is blackmailing entire world on the pretext of their socalled alliance to fight terrorism. Pakistan's military dictatorship cannot be trusted. Pakistan's military dictatorship can use nuclear power to protect its evil designs and plans to conquer the world in the light of Quranic verses which they interpret on the basis of guidelines provided by their 'Religious Consultants' called Tablighi Jamat which in turn is a RELIGIOUS CULT of modern times busy in promoting evil designs of WAHABIAT (Saudi brand of Islam). Some of the verses which are currently serving as 'leading principles' for Pakistan's military dictatorship and ISI for promoting Hory War(Jihad) are as follows:

Qur'an 5:33: "The punishment for those who wage war against Allah and His Prophet and perpetrate mischief [reject Islam or oppose its goals] in the land, is to murder them, to hang them, to mutilate them, or banish them. Such is their disgrace. They will not escape the fire, suffering constantly."

Explanation: In view of this particular verse, Pakistan's military dictatorship intends to crush all those elements which are against Allah (here reference is particularly made to Allah of Muslims and not Christian God) as indicated by the religious scholars of Tablighi Jamat. The terms 'murder', 'hang', 'mutilate' and 'banish' show the extremism preached by Tablighi Jamat openly in broad day light while no one is empowered to say or object against such an attitude.

Qur'an 9:88 "The Messenger and those who believe with him, strive hard and fight with their wealth and lives in Allah's Cause."

Explanation: The Tablighi Jamat exploits the interpretation of this particular verse to justify the need of spending money and ofcourse donating money for the socalled just cause of 'fight' against Christians, Jews and Hindus. Here fight is understood as aggression and killing. There is nothing like 'defence' or 'self-protection' in the light of interpretations accepted and propagated by Tablighi Jamat for any Quranic verse discussing the topic of Jihad.

Qur'an 9:5 "Fight and kill the disbelievers wherever you find them, take them captive, harass them, lie in wait and ambush them using every stratagem of war."

Explanation: The Tablighi Jamat advocates legitimacy of kidnappings, harrassment and extortion of money by way of ransom in lieu of this particular verse of Quran. The military dictatorship of Pakistan follows the same interpretation since it is certified by Tablighi Jamat under the auspices of Saudi Kingdom.

Qur'an 9:111 "The Believers fight in Allah's Cause, they slay and are slain, kill and are killed."

Explanation: This verse is interpreted in the same spirit of 'killing' and 'murdering' by the Tablighi Jamat as followed by Pakistan's military dictatorship.

Qur'an 8:39 "Fight them until all opposition ends and all submit to Allah."

Explanation: Tablighi Jamat applies this verse to Pakistan's internal conflicts related to freedom movements in Pakhtoonistan (NWFP), Baluchistan,

Sidhudesh and Jinnahpur (Karachi) whereby Tablighi Jamat justifies killing of people of provinces other than Punjab for the sake of glory of Islam and rectification of human sins committed by people of Pakhtoonistan (NWFP), Baluchistan, Sidhudesh and Jinnahpur (Karachi). All military operations undertaken by Pakistan Army in Pakhtoonistan (NWFP), Baluchistan, Sidhudesh and Jinnahpur (Karachi) in connivance with ISI are justified in lieu of this interpretation by Tablighi Jamat. As the first Fascists of Islam like Abu Bakr (the first Muslim Caliph) and Omar bin Khattab (the second Muslim Caliph) exercised their military strength to persecute the supporters of Ali (son-in-law of Muhammad SA), Tablighi Jamat recommends the same strategy to control the people of Pakhtoonistan (NWFP), Baluchistan, Sidhudesh and Jinnahpur (Karachi) and Shias in Pakistan.

Qur'an 9:14 "Fight them and Allah will punish them by your hands, lay them low, and cover them with shame. He will help you over them."

Explanation: The Tablighi Jamat being a Religious Cult advocates use of power to insult the people living in Pakhtoonistan (NWFP), Baluchistan, Sidhudesh and Jinnahpur (Karachi) and Shias living in Pakistan. This is the reason why the military dictatorship of Pakistan finds the acts of insult and persecution of people living in Pakhtoonistan (NWFP), Baluchistan, Sidhudesh and Jinnahpur (Karachi) and Shias living in Pakistan according to Islamic teachings (sponsored by Wahabiat brand of Islam institutionalized by Saudi Kingdom).

Qur'an 8:65 "O Prophet, urge the faithful to fight. If there are twenty among you with determination they will vanquish two hundred; if there are a hundred then they will slaughter a thousand unbelievers, for the infidels are a people devoid of understanding."

Explanation: The Tablighi Jamat used this particular verse like 'National Anthem' during the days of Afghan war against Soviet Union. Since, at that time, Pakistan needed a cheap fighting force to expel Soviet Union out of Afghanistan, fighters were recruited in the name of socalled 'Islamic Jihad'. Tablighi Jamat sent thousands of its workers to NWFP and Afghanistan in order to propagate the concept of Holy War (Jihad) by repeatedly quoting this particular verse.

Qur'an 8:12 "I shall terrorize the infidels. So wound their bodies and incapacitate them because they oppose Allah and His Apostle."

Explanation: This verse was also exploited by Tablighi Jamat in similar pattern to 'boost' the confidence of Pakistan military and the cheap fighting force during Afghan war.

Qur'an 8:57 "If you gain mastery over them in battle, inflict such a defeat as would terrorize them, so that they would learn a lesson and be warned."

Explanation: This verse was quoted by Tablighi Jamat more frequently when certain areas under the control of Soviet Union in Afghanistan were captured by Taliban (Army of Muslim Hypocrites sponsored by ISI). Tablighi Jamat's religious scholars allowed the Muslim butchers to kill and murder those Soviet soldiers who were either alive at the time of capture or who surrendered themselves. Tablighi Jamat advocated the need of killing of Prisoners of War in the light of this particular verse.

Qur'an 8:67 "It is not fitting for any prophet to have prisoners until he has made a great slaughter in the land."

Explanation: Tablighi Jamat interpreted this particular verse in the same spirit as above.

Qur'an 8:7 "Allah wished to confirm the truth by His words: 'Wipe the infidels out to the last."

Explanation: Tablighi Jamat advocated the need of killing of non-Muslims on authority of this particular verse on several occasions. People dont understand exactly the purpose of propagating of such misleading interpretations by Tablighi Jamat around the world and in Pakistan.

Qur'an 8:12 "Your Lord inspired the angels with the message: 'I am with you. Give firmness to the Believers. I will terrorize the unbelievers. Therefore smite them on their necks and every joint and incapacitate them. Strike off their heads and cut off each of their fingers and toes."

Explanation: This is a very famous verse fully exploited by Tablighi Jamat in order to motivate its followers (or say Cult members) to kill and murder Christians, Jews and Hindus.

Qur'an 8:15 "Believers, when you meet unbelieving infidels in battle while you are marching for war, never turn your backs to them. If any turns his back on such a day, unless it be in a stratagem of war, a maneuver to rally his side, he draws on himself the wrath of Allah, and his abode is Hell, an evil refuge!"

Explanation: This verse was also used as an effective weapon by Tablighi Jamat to motivate thousands of Talibans during Afghan war against Soviet Union.

Qur'an 8:59 "The infidels should not think that they can escape. Prepare against them whatever arms and weaponry you can muster so that you may terrorize them. They are your enemy and Allah's enemy."

Explanation: This is also a very famous verse fully exploited by Tablighi Jamat in order to motivate its followers (or say Cult members) to kill and murder Christians, Jews and Hindus.

Qur'an 8:60 "And make ready against the infidels all of the power you can, including steeds of war to threaten the enemy of Allah and your enemy. And whatever you spend in Allah's Cause shall be repaid unto you." [Another translation reads:] "Prepare against them whatever arms and cavalry you can muster that you may strike terror in the enemies of Allah, and others besides them."

Qur'an 8:71 "He will give you mastery over them."

Explanation: These are also very much quoted verses fully exploited by Tablighi Jamat in order to motivate its followers (or say Cult members) to kill and murder Christians, Jews and Hindus.

Qur'an 33:22 "Among the Believers are men who have been true to their covenant with Allah and have gone out for Jihad (holy fighting). Some have completed their vow to extreme and have been martyred fighting and dying in His Cause, and some are waiting, prepared for death in battle."

Explanation: Tablighi Jamat contemplates the legitimacy of 'suicide bombing' in lieu of this particular verse. In the opinion of Tablighi Jamat, 'some have completed their vow' refers to those Muslims who took part in suicide bombings against Jews and Christians while 'some are waiting' refers to those who are ready and willing to act in line with their colleagues i.e. to commit suicide attacks on Christians, Jews and Hindus.

Qur'an 4:95 "Not equal are those believers who sit at home and receive no injurious hurt, and those who strive hard, fighting Jihad in Allah's Cause with their wealth and lives. Allah has granted a rank higher to those who strive hard, fighting Jihad with their wealth and bodies to those who sit. Allah prefers Jihadists who strive hard and fight above those who sit home. He has distinguished his fighters with a huge reward."

Explanation: Tablighi Jamat openly quotes this verse to provoke those people who refuse to take part in socalled relgious activities of Tablighi Jamat.

Qur'an 47:4 "So, when you clash with the unbelieving Infidels in battle (fighting Jihad in Allah's Cause), smite their necks until you overpower them, killing and wounding many of them. At length, when you have thoroughly subdued them, bind them firmly, making (them) captives. Thereafter either generosity or ransom (them based upon what benefits Islam) until the war lays down its burdens. Thus are you commanded by Allah to continue carrying out Jihad against the unbelieving infidels until they submit to Islam."

Explanation: This is also a very famous verse fully exploited by Tablighi Jamat in order to motivate its followers (or say Cult members) to kill and murder Christians, Jews and Hindus.

Qur'an 2:216 "Jihad (holy fighting in Allah's Cause) is ordained for you (Muslims), though you dislike it. But it is possible that you dislike a thing which is good for you, and like a thing which is bad for you. But Allah knows, and you know not."

Explanation: This is also a very famous verse fully exploited by Tablighi Jamat in order to motivate its followers (or say Cult members) to kill and murder Christians, Jews and Hindus.

Qur'an 47:33 "Believers, obey Allah, and obey the Messenger. Do not falter; become faint-hearted, or weak-kneed, crying for peace."

Explanation: This particular verse is very useful too. Tablighi Jamat takes credit of being on the righteous path, hence, motivates its Cult members to follow its guidelines in lieu of this verse. 'Obey' is defined in the sense that the followers should obey the commandments of religious scholars of Tablighi Jamat.

Qur'an 9:3 "Allah is not bound by any contract or treaty with non-Muslims, nor is His Apostle."

Explanation: Here, the Tablighi Jamat disallows the concept of entering into any form of agreement of whatever nature. Tablighi Jamat does not consider any truce with Christians or Jews or Hindus as any binding. It is for this reason that the Pakistan's military dictatorship always refuses to enter into any dialogue with India on political issues and does not hesitate to break all agreed terms.

Qur'an 8:58 "If you apprehend treachery from any group on the part of a people (with whom you have a treaty), retaliate by breaking off (relations) with them. The infidels should not think they can bypass (Islamic law or the punishment of Allah). Surely they cannot escape."

Explanation: Tablighi Jamat quotes this verse to justify non-compliance and default as legitimate. Pakistan's Army accordingly behaves in the spirit of this particular verse as taught by Tablighi Jamat.

Qur'an 48:11 "The desert Arabs who lagged behind [in fighting] will say to you (Muhammad): 'We were engaged in (looking after) our flocks and our families.' We [Allah] have prepared for them a Blazing Fire!"

Explanation: Tablighi Jamat quotes this verse as an open threat for those who refuse to participate in the activities of Tablighi Jamat.

Qur'an 48:17 "There is no blame for the blind, nor is it a sin for the lame, nor on one ill if he joins not in the fighting. But he who retreats, (Allah) will punish him with a painful doom."

Explanation: Tablighi Jamat quotes this verse as an open threat for those who refuse to participate in the activities of Tablighi Jamat.

Qur'an 4:77 "Have you not seen those to whom it was said: Withhold your hands from fighting, perform the prayer and pay the zakat. But when orders for fighting were issued, a party of them feared men as they ought to have feared Allah. They say: 'Our Lord, why have You ordained fighting for us, why have You made war compulsory?'"

Explanation: Tablighi Jamat quotes this verse as an open threat for those who refuse to participate in the activities of Tablighi Jamat.

Qur'an 4:88 "What is the matter with you that you are divided about the Hypocrites? Allah has cast them back (causing their disbelief). Would you guide those whom Allah has thrown out of the way? For those whom Allah has thrown aside and led astray, never shall they find the way."

Explanation: This is also a very famous verse fully exploited by Tablighi Jamat in order to motivate its followers (or say Cult members) to kill and murder Christians, Jews and Hindus.

Qur'an 4:89 "They wish that you would reject Faith, as they have, and thus be on the same footing: Do not be friends with them until they leave their homes in Allah's Cause. But [and this is a hell of a but...] if they turn back from Islam, becoming renegades, seize them and kill them wherever you find them."

Explanation: This is also a very famous verse fully exploited by Tablighi Jamat in order to motivate its followers (or say Cult members) to kill and murder Christians, Jews and Hindus.

Qur'an 47:20 "Those who believe say, 'How is it that no surah was sent down (for us)?' But when a categorical [decisive or uncompromising] surah is revealed, and fighting and war (Jihad, holy fighting in Allah's Cause) are ordained, you will see those with diseased hearts looking at you (Muhammad) fainting unto death. Therefore, woe unto them!"

Explanation: This is also a very famous verse fully exploited by Tablighi Jamat in order to motivate its followers (or say Cult members) to kill and murder Christians, Jews and Hindus.

Qur'an 47:21 "Were they to obey, showing their obedience in modest speech, after the matter (of preparation for Jihad) had been determined for them, it would have been better...Such men are cursed by Allah. He has made them deaf, dumb and blind."

Explanation: Tablighi Jamat quotes this verse as an open threat for those who refuse to participate in the activities of Tablighi Jamat.

Qur'an 9:90 "And there were among the wandering desert Arabs men who made excuses and came to claim exemption (from the battle). Those who lied to Allah and His Messenger sat at home. Soon will a grievous torment seize them."

Explanation: Tablighi Jamat quotes this verse as an open threat for those who refuse to participate in the activities of Tablighi Jamat.

Qur'an 9:93 "The (complaint) is against those who claim exemption [from fighting] while they are rich. They prefer to stay with the (women) who remain behind (at home). Allah has sealed their hearts. They are content to be useless. Say: 'Present no excuses: we shall not believe you.' It is your actions that Allah and His Messenger will observe. They will swear to you by Allah, when you return hoping that you might leave them alone. So turn away from them, for they are unclean, an abomination, and Hell is their dwelling-place, a fitting recompense for them."

Explanation: Tablighi Jamat quotes this verse as an open threat for those who refuse to participate in the activities of Tablighi Jamat.

Qur'an 9:97 "The Arabs of the desert are the worst in unbelief and hypocrisy, and most fitted to be in ignorance of the command which Allah hath sent down to His Messenger. Some of the Bedouins look upon their payments (for Allah's Cause) as a fine and wish disasters to fall on you (so that they might not have to pay). Yet on them be the disaster of evil."

Explanation: Tablighi Jamat quotes this verse as an open threat for those who refuse to participate in the activities of Tablighi Jamat.

Qur'an 9:101 "Among the desert Arabs are hypocrites. They, like the people of Medina are obstinate in hypocrisy. We know them. Twice shall We punish them, and in addition they shall be brought back to a horrible torment."

Explanation: Tablighi Jamat quotes this verse as an open threat for those who refuse to participate in the activities of Tablighi Jamat.

Qur'an 9:120 "It is not fitting for the people of Medina and the Bedouin Arabs to refuse to follow Allah's Messenger (Muhammad when fighting in Allah's Cause), nor to prefer their own lives to his life. They suffer neither thirst nor fatigue in Allah's Cause, no do they go without reward. They do not take steps to raise the anger of disbelievers, nor inflict any injury upon an enemy without it being written to their credit as a deed of righteousness."

Explanation: This is also a very famous verse fully exploited by Tablighi Jamat in order to motivate its followers (or say Cult members) to kill and murder Christians, Jews and Hindus.

Qur'an 8:72 "Those who accepted Islam and left their homes to fight in Allah's Cause with their possessions and persons, and those who gave them shelter and aided them are your allies. You are only called to protect Muslims who fight."

Explanation: Tablighi Jamat advocates the importance of support for the terrorists by its followers in lieu of this particular verse.

Qur'an 8:73 "The infidels aid one another. Unless you do the same there will be anarchy in the land. Those who accepted Islam and left their homes to fight in Allah's Cause are good Muslims."

Explanation: Tablighi Jamat advocates the importance of support for the terrorists by its followers in lieu of this particular verse.

I was member of Tablighi Jamat from 1984 to 1991. During this period, I was able to penetrate into the inner circle of Tablighi Jamat so much so that I was able to talk to Abdul Wahab (the main leader), Maulana Saeed Ahmed Khan (late), Maulana Jamshed, Maulana Muhammad Ahmed (Bahawalpur), Mufti Zainul Abedin (Faisalabad), Maulana Farooq, Ibrahim Abdul Jabbar (Karachi), Amin (Karachi), Yameen (Karachi) and several other similar scholars of this notorious group. I dont know who many of them have died todate since I had to leave Pakistan due to threats by ISI immediately after 1990 on my return from Bangladesh where I had spent some time with Tablighi Jamat of Bangladesh in Dhaka at Kakrail mosque. My experience with Tablighi Jamat allowed me to visit various cantonment areas in different parts of Pakistan. I got opportunity to meet with several ex-Army and serving officers who were members of Tablighi Jamat. Since my attire was purely identical to that of a worker of Tablighi Jamat and myself being very fluent in preaching of Islam, it was rather a golden chance on my part to closely evaluate the functions and strategies of Tablighi Jamat. To my surprise, there were several facts about the role of Tablighi Jamat and its aims which came to my attention. Some of them were:

1. TO DESTROY USA, ISRAEL AND INDIA IN COMPLIANCE WITH CERTAIN VERSES OF QURAN WHEREBY SUCH DESTRUCTION WAS A DIVINE COMMANDMENT BY ALLAH (GOD);

2. TO BRAIN-WASH NON-MUSLIMS THROUGH PERSONAL MOTIVATION AND PERSUASIVE LECTURES (DAWAT) ENABLING THEM TO EMBRACE ISLAM;

3. TO TRAIN SPECIAL GROUPS OF PREACHERS TO BE SENT TO ALL IMPORTANT COUNTRIES IN THE WORLD WHERE THEY SHOULD BE ABLE TO ACT AS PREACHERS IN ORDER TO FIND MUSLIMS LIVING IN THOSE COUNTRIES SO AS TO MOTIVATE THEM TO RISE AGAINST CHRISTIANS, JEWS AND INFIDELS LIVING IN THOSE COUNTRIES;

4. TO AVOID DISTRIBUTION OF ANY WRITE-UPS OR BOOKS OR CASSETTES BUT TO EXPLORE ALL POSSIBLE MEANS OF SPEECH;

5. TO SELECT MUSLIMS LIVING IN SUCH COUNTRIES AND SENDING THEM TO PAKISTAN FOR A 4-MONTH TRAINING CALLED 'LEARNING SESSIONS IN THE PATH OF ALLAH';

6. TO PROVIDE NECESSARY FUNDS FOR SUCH INTERNATIONAL TRIPS OF PREACHERS OF TABLIGHI JAMAT (FUNDS WERE PAID BY ISI);

7. TO LAUNCH A MASSIVE RELIGIOUS CAMPAIGN AROUND THE WORLD THROUGH « POWER OF SPEECH » CALLED 'DAWAT' TO WIN THE HEARTS OF ALL MUSLIMS IN ORDER TO MAKE THEM UNDERSTAND THAT QURAN WANTS ALL MUSLIMS TO RISE WITH AN AIM TO CONVERT THE ENTIRE WORLD POPULATION INTO MUSLIMS;

8. TO REFRAIN FROM PARTICIPATION IN ANY POLITICAL MOVEMENT IN PAKISTAN SINCE SUCH POLITICAL MOVEMENTS ARE UNISLAMIC AND AGAINST THE DOCTORINE OF TRUE MUSLIM/ISLAMIC LEADERSHIP TERMED AS « KHILAFAT »;

9. TO REFRAIN FROM READING OF ANY WRITTEN LITERATURE OR NEWSPAPERS OR WATCHING TV ETC SINCE SUCH ACTS ARE TOTALLY FORBIDDEN IN ISLAM;

10. TO KEEP DISTANCE FROM THOSE FAMILY MEMBERS WHO DO NOT SHOW THEIR RESPECT TOWARDS THE WORK OF TABLIGHI JAMAT;

11. TO ORGANIZE REGULAR MEETINGS IN MOSQUES TO EVALU-
ATE PROGRESS OF WORK IN THE AREA AND TO REPORT BACK
TO THE MAIN « MARKAZ » (Headquarter) OF THE CITY;

12. TO PREPARE NEW TEAMS OF ENGLISH AND ARABIC SPEAKING
PREACHERS WHO SHOULD BE ABLE TO TALK TO FOREIGN
MUSLIMS COMING TO PAKISTAN EITHER AS STUDENTS OF
RELIGIOUS SCHOOLS IN PAKISTAN OR TO LEARN RELIGION
OF ISLAM UNDER THE BANNER OF TABLIGHI JAMAT IN
ORDER TO MENTALLY PREPARE THEM FOR A FIGHT IN THE
PATH OF ALLAH;

13. TO TARGET NEW MUSLIM GENERATION LIVING IN USA, UK,
AUSTRALIA, AFRICA AND INDIA IN ORDER TO CONVEY TO
THEM SPECIAL MESSAGE ABOUT « FIGHT IN THE NOBLE PATH
OF ALLAH » EITHER THROUGH SWORD OR WORD;

14. TO OBTAIN ALL POSSIBLE FINANCIAL AS WELL AS MORAL SUP-
PORT FROM MUSLIMS LIVING IN MIDDLE EAST IN THE NAME
OF PREACHING OF ISLAM;

15. TO ORGANIZE LARGE CONGREGATIONS IN PAKISTAN AS
WELL AS ABROAD TO BRAIN-WASH PEOPLE (ABOUT JIHAD-
HOLY WAR);

Tablighi Jamat (Pakistan Chapter) headquartered in Raiwind-Lahore under the
sponsorship of ISI has been propagating the above Quranic verses in negative
manner by brain-washing young men from different parts of Pakistan, United
Kingdom, USA, Australia and the Middle East. The above verses of Quran which
relate to the time of Holy Prophet SA (about 1500 years ago) are interpreted by
Tablighi Jamat in the context of destruction of Christians, Jews and Hindus living in this world. The new generation of Muslims is being brain-washed in the
name of 'Enjoining Good & Forbidding Bad' by Tablighi Jamat. They have been
working since last 80 years, hence, it is not easy to crush their organized network
either through newly adopted security measures at airports or vulnerable locations. The poison of Tablighi Jamat has already spread like AIDS in the veins of
young Muslim generation living in USA, United Kingdom, Australia and the
Middle East apart from different areas of Pakistan.

With the socalled 'spiritual' support and struggle of Tablighi Jamat, Pakistan has turned out to be a Fascist State in recent years. The main characteristics of such Facist state as observed are as follows:

a) Promotion of Punjabi Culture in the name of Pakistan Nationalism

Pakistan has become property of one province known as PUNJAB which houses largest population of the country while the corrupt military dictatorship also belongs to this particular province. Henceforth, the backward culture of this province emanating from the dirty villages and red light areas born decades ago are portrayed as culture of Pakistan. This act of exhibiting Punjab's local culture is termed as National Culture which is also one of the main elements of modern fascism. Pakistan's disintegration can pave way to free the hijacked cultures of people demanding Pakhtoonistan, Baluchistan, Sindhudesh and Jinnahpur.

b) Violation of Human Rights

Pakistan is a place where there is no judicial system. All Punjabi judges are posted every where in the country who are either corrupt by birth in view of their parenthood crisis or have been bought by the military dictatorship. This is an important sign of fascism whereby the rule of law is replaced by a regime of military dictatorship. Extra-judicial killings are common in Pakistan and this fact is very well known to the entire world. Although, the military leadership refuses to confess their sins, yet, they have no answers in response to the statistics indicating deaths of several thousand people in the last 25 years in police or military custody. Prisoners are treated as animals while the Army Generals sitting at the General Headquarters are enjoying their soft beds along with the prostitutes hailing from their beloved land called Punjab. The act of violating human rights is glaring example of fascism in the modern world. Only Pakistan's disintegration can remove the hurdles in the way of ethical prosperity of people living in South Asia.

c) Creation of artificial enemies or scapegoats

The military dictatorship in Pakistan along with their puppet organization known as Inter-Services Intelligence (ISI) is always looking for scapegoats to hide their own sins. This act contemplates that the military dictatorship of Punjab is hiding thousands of skeletons in thousands of closets. These corrupt officials of Pakistan's corrupt army are engaged in conspiracy of distracting public attention from the main political issues. Recent murder of Akbar Bugti, freedom fighter of Baluchistan was yet another attempt to destroy the will of people and giving them absurd impression of facilitation of national security and elimination of internal terrorism. The act of diverting the people's attention is itself an evidence of fascism which was quite common among the fascist regimes. If Pakistan is dis- integrated today and as such divided into 5 parts, the consistent exercise of hypo- critic distraction by the military dictatorship shall be eliminated forever.

d) Supremacy of Military Rule

The military dictatorship of Pakistan has also caused supremacy of Military Rule instead of Rule of Law. Pakistan's former Justice Nasir Aslam Zahid, who had served on the Supreme Court and had been Chief Justice of Sindh, openly con- fessed that when the Supreme Court judges went to take their oath of office under the new military government in 2000, they were presented with empty pieces of paper from which to read. The higher court judges had been ordered on January 19 to take a new oath under a Provisional Constitutional Order, some three months after General Pervez Musharraf, the brutal military dictator, had taken power and scrapped the constitution. According to Justice Zahid, when they were to take the oath the following day, the registrar gave the judges blank forms from which they were to recite. Egged on by Justice Irshad Hassan Khan, who then became chief justice, they took their oaths without seeing any text. This has exposed the face of real Pakistan which does not deserve any more existence on this world map. Army personnel had surrounded his house while a colonel kept him in his chair, and out of the bench. It seems that the army was trying to spare him the indignity of the oath-taking pantomime. The story would be funny were it told on a comedy programme and not by a retired judge. Unfortunately, it only serves to remind us of how Pakistan's judiciary was destroyed over the last half-century. Whenever Pakistan's top judges have been faced with a critical deci- sion on the constitution or military rule, they have gone to the door of General Headquarters in order to seek instructions. From this point on, a so-called doc- trine (Doctrine of Necessity), rather than the constitution, national or interna- tional law, became the basis for every decision on the legitimacy of a military takeover. With one blow, Chief Justice Munir destroyed the foundations of con- stitutional rule in Pakistan. In one move, he opened wide the door for the army to walk into government any time it wanted. History and the court both repeated themselves in 2000, when Zafar Ali Shah challenged the constitutionality of the October 12 military coup of the year before. At the time that General Musharraf took power he appeared to have strong political backing. Still, when the chief jus- tice was asked about the constitutionality of the coup, he said that any petition coming to the court would be decided on its merits. One day before the Supreme

Court was due to make its decision, off he went to headquarters for a briefing. (This is the same guy who goaded bemused fellow judges with their blank slips of paper on January 20 to "hurry up, take the oath [because] we have to save the country".) The following day the full bench judgment not only upheld the coup but went so far as to give General Musharraf unlimited power to amend the constitution as he pleased. The doctrine of necessity was pulled out and shook around one more time. Some in Pakistan's legal circles claim that this decision was literally written outside the court and handed to the judges to pronounce without even having had time to read it properly. Pakistan's poodle judiciary has been taught and learnt its lessons well. On but a few occasions in the last half-century has the Supreme Court declined to use the doctrine of necessity, and even then the attendant circumstances have meant that its actions were meaningless. By subordinating itself to the military, Pakistan's judiciary long since passed over the threshold of reality and into a fantasy land. It is a land in which you can read other people's judgments as if they are your own. It is a land in which you can swear on a spotless piece of paper. It is a land in which you must wear a blank expression and carry around an empty mind. It is a land in which the law exists in a vacuum. This is nothing but another evidence of fascism in Pakistan under control of a military dictator. Hence, disintegration of Pakistan has also become an urgent necessity under the same Doctrine of Necessity.

Another Approach

The disintegration of Pakistan has become inevitable because the circumstances currently existing in Pakistan are very similar to 1971. The reasons responsible for the division of Pakistan in 1971 will still be valid for yet another division of Pakistan in almost 5 parts this time. During the time of East Pakistan, the Bangladesh Liberation War (MuktiJuddho) was fighting for the rights of Bengali Muslims who were economically, socially and politically persecuted by the military dictatorship of Punjabi army. Just like that we can see today that Baluchistan Liberation Army and Sindh Liberation Army are also fighting for the rights of people of Baluchistan and Sindh respectively. The fight for liberation of Pakhtoonistan is also going on in parallel terms in the North West Frontier Province of today's Pakistan. It is a historic fact that armed conflict between West Pakistan (now Pakistan) through the military dictators of that time and East Pakistan (now Bangladesh) through their freedom fighters that lasted for roughly nine months, from 26 March until 16 December 1971 resulted in Bangladesh's independence from Pakistan. This was a great achievement on the part of Bengali Muslims who had realized that the concept of Pakistan was not more than a mockery of facts.

Recent murder of Nawab Akbar Bugti by Pakistan Army on August 26, 2006 proves this argument.

During the Partition of India which was indeed a conspiracy of great standard committed by the then politicians of United India in connivance with the selfish Muslim leaders including Jinnah, Pakistan, as a country, gained independence on 14 August 1947 following the end of British rule over South Asian countries. The division was made based on religion despite the fact that Jinnah was a man without any religious background or knowledge about Islam. Jinnah was a hired barrister to fight the case of Pakistan. Pakistan was created out of huge Muslim majority territories in the West and East, and India was created out of the vast Hindu majority regions in the centre. The Western zone was popularly (and for a period of time, also officially) called West Pakistan and the Eastern zone (modern-day Bangladesh) was called East Bengal and later, East Pakistan. The capital of Pakistan was established in Karachi in West Pakistan and then moved to Islamabad in 1958.

West Pakistan (consisting of four provinces: Punjab, Sindh, Balochistan and North-West Frontier Province) dominated the divided country politically and received more money from the common budget than the more populous East.

Year	Spending on West Pakistan (in billion Rupees)	Spending on East Pakistan (in billion Rupees)	Amount spent on East as percentage of West
1950/51–54/55	11.29	5.24	46.4
1955/56–59/60	16.55	5.24	31.7
1960/61–64/65	33.55	14.04	41.8
1965/66–69/70	51.95	21.41	41.2
Total	113.34	45.93	40.5

*   *Source: Reports of the Advisory Panels for the Fourth Five Year Plan 1970–75, Vol. I, published by the Planning Commission of Pakistan.*

Between 1948 and 1960, East Pakistan produced 70% of all of Pakistan's exports, while it only received 25% of import earnings. In 1948 (shortly after independence from Britain), East Pakistan had 11 textile mills while the West had 9. In 1971, the number of textile mills in the West had grown to 150 while that in the East had only gone up to 26. Furthermore, 2.6 billion dollars' (in 1971 exchange rates) worth of resources were transferred over time from East Pakistan to West Pakistan. It was widely felt in East Pakistan that much of the income generated by the east was diverted towards fighting wars in Kashmir. Similar to this situation, today Punjab is exploiting resources of Baluchistan and North West Frontier Province. Today, People from Baluchistan and NWFP dont have clean drinking water, proper roads, electricity, education, employment opportunities, participation in national politics, development of infra-structure or even proper housing. This is an evidence that Punjab's military dictatorship is yet again doing what they did in early 1970s which caused the inception of Bangladesh. The innovation this time is called « terrorism » whereby Punjab's military dictatorship which is administering Inter-Services Intelligence (ISI) wants to implicate Baluchistan, NWFP and Sindh in false cases of terrorism in order to show to their American masters that these provinces are responsible for harbouring terrorists and organizing terrorism although the fact is totally reverse. ISI is now acting on behalf of Punjab's military dictatorship to propagate a false impression that people from NWFP and Baluchistan are friends of Osama and Taliban while people from Sindh are supporting Indian aggression in Pakistan. In line with a well-organized plan of action, ISI has been busy in sponsoring terrorist activities all over the world in connivance with the international terrorist networks. Hence, the blame is being put on people of NWFP, Baluchistan and Sindh while ISI is itself responsible for promoting Islamic militancy all over the world in an organized manner.

Coming back to the point, although East Pakistan was the majority province in terms of population, political power remained firmly in the hands of West Pakistanis, specifically the hatred-filled Punjabis. Since a straightforward system of representation based on population would have concentrated political power in East Pakistan, the West Pakistani military dictatorship came up with the scheme of "One Unit", where all of West Pakistan was considered one province. This was solely to counterbalance the East wing's votes. Ironically, after the East broke away to form Bangladesh, the Punjab insisted that politics in the rump West Pakistan now be decided on the basis of a straightforward vote, since Punjabis were more numerous than the other groups, such as Sindhis, Pathans, or Balochs. After the assassination of Liaquat Ali Khan, political power began to be concentrated in the President of Pakistan, and eventually, the military. The nominal elected chief executive, the Prime Minister, was frequently sacked by the establishment, acting through the President. East Pakistanis noticed that whenever one of them, such as Khawaja Nazimuddin, Muhammad Ali Bogra, or Huseyn Shaheed Suhrawardy were elected Prime Minister of Pakistan, they were swiftly deposed by the largely West Pakistani establishment. The military dictatorships of Ayub Khan and Yahya Khan, both West Pakistanis, only heightened such feelings. Finally, when Sheikh Mujib's Awami League won a clear majority in the elections of 1970, the West Pakistan establishment refused to allow Mujib to form a government. This finally convinced the East that they would never get their rightful political rights in a joint Pakistan and that independence was the only way out. This is exactly what is happening in today's Pakistan. Political leaders belonging to NWFP, Baluchistan and Sindh are regarded as « separatists » and « anti-Pakistan » while the military dictatorship is termed as « loyal savers of Pakistan ». I guess, time has come that history should repeat itself. Pakistan should be further divided into 5 more parts to make it clear to the entire world that dictatorships dont have long life. I am confident that Pakistan will never celebrate its 60th Independence Day. 14th August 2006 was Pakistan's last birthday.

Back to the discussion. Close ties existed between East Pakistan and West Bengal, one of the Indian states bordering Bangladesh, as both were composed mostly of Bengalis. West Pakistan viewed East Pakistani links with India unfavourably as relations between India and Pakistan had been very poor since independence. In 1948, Mohammad Ali Jinnah declared in Dhaka (then usually spelt Dacca in English) that "Urdu, and only Urdu" would be the sole official language for all of Pakistan. This proved highly controversial, since Urdu was a language that was only spoken in the West by Muhajir and in the East by Biharis. The majority groups in West Pakistan spoke Punjabi and Sindhi, while Bangla was spoken by the majority of East Pakistanis. The language controversy eventually reached a point where East Pakistan revolted. Several students and civilians lost their lives in a police crackdown on February 21, 1952. The day is revered in Bangladesh and in West Bengal as the Language Martyrs' Day. Later, in memory of the 1952 killings, UNESCO declared February 21 as the International Mother Language Day. The deaths led to bitter feelings among East Pakistanis, and they were a major factor in the push for independence. Punjab's military dictatorship still hates Urdu and Urdu-speaking people of Pakistan living in urban areas of Sindh for the specific reason that the whole world had condemned them for the atrocities committed by them in East Pakistan. The Army Generals of Punjab's military dictatorship had become 'Gods' in East Pakistan at that time whereby they killed Bengali Muslims to exhibit their hatred for them. People of Punjab may be good but their Army turned out to be an arrogant force ready to crush humanity at every cost.

The already tense situation was further aggravated by a tropical cyclone that struck East Pakistan in 1970. It was a particularly devastating year as the deadliest cyclone on record—the 1970 Bhola cyclone—struck Bangladesh claiming nearly half a million lives. The apathy of West Pakistan leadership and its failure in responding quickly was a further platform for the Awami League, that capitalised on this tragedy. The Pakistan Army failed to do relief work of any significance to alleviate the problem, which further antagonised the already estranged Bengali populace. Just like what they did in 1970, this time also in 2005, the same military dictatorship also failed to do what was required of them for the Earthquake victims of Kashmir. History has already proven what the military dictatorship did in East Pakistan and those who remember history should also see that the same Punjabi military dictatorship neglected rehabilitation work for the Kashmiri people because Punjab's military dictatorship does not consider Kashmiris different from Bengalis.

Sheikh Mujibur Rahman who had signed an official declaration on 25th March 1971 that read:

"Today Bangladesh is a sovereign and independent country. On Thursday night West Pakistani armed forces suddenly attacked the police barracks at Razarbagh and the EPR headquarters at Pilkhana in Dhaka. Many innocent and unarmed have been killed in Dhaka city and other places of Bangladesh. Violent clashes between EPR and Police on the one hand and the armed forces of Pakistan on the other, are going on. The Bengalis are fighting the enemy with great courage for an independent Bangladesh. May God aid us in our fight for freedom. Joy Bangla."

(Source: "The History of the Liberation Movement in Bangladesh" by J. S. Gupta)

A telegram reached some students in Chittagong. They realized the message could be broadcast from Agrabad Station of Radio Pakistan. The message was translated to Bangla by Dr Manjula Anwar. They failed to secure permission from higher authorities to broadcast the message. They crossed Kalurghat Bridge into an area controlled by East Bengal Regiment under Major Ziaur Rahman. Bengali soldiers guarded the station as engineers prepared for transmission. At 19:45 on 26 March 1971, Major Ziaur Rahman broadcast another announcement of the declaration of independence on behalf of Sheikh Mujibur which is as follows.

"This is Shadhin Bangla Betar Kendro. I, Major Ziaur Rahman, at the direction of Bangobondhu Mujibur Rahman, hereby declare that the independent People's Republic of Bangladesh has been established. At his direction, I have taken command as the temporary Head of the Republic. In the name of Sheikh Mujibur Rahman, I call upon all Bengalis to rise against the attack by the West Pakistani Army. We shall fight to the last to free our Motherland. By the grace of Allah, victory is ours. Joy Bangla."

Kalurghat Radio Station's transmission capability was limited. The message was picked up by a Japanese ship in Bay of Bengal and then re-transmitted by Radio Australia and later the British Broadcasting Corporation. 26 March 1971 is hence considered the official Independence Day and according to all Bangladeshi sources, the name Bangladesh was in effect henceforth.

Time has now come to hear similar words from political leaderships of NWFP, Baluchistan and Sindh. ISI has already hijacked Jinnah's Pakistan to make it a TERRORIST TRAINING CAMP. The political leaders of NWFP, Baluchistan and Sindh should get up and immediately approach United Nations for a voluntary dissolution of Pakistan to eliminate terrorism without any bloodshed as happened when political events gathered momentum in 1970s whereby the stage was set for a clash between the Pakistan Army and the insurgents which finally caused deaths of several thousand Bengali Muslims.

Though the United Nations condemned the human rights violations in East Pakistan (Bangladesh), it failed to defuse the situation politically before the start of the war. The Security Council assembled on December 4 to discuss the volatile situation in South Asia. USSR vetoed the resolution twice. After lengthy discussions on December 7, the General Assembly promptly adopted by a majority resolution calling for an "immediate cease-fire and withdrawal of troops." The United States on December 12 requested that the Security Council be reconvened. However by the time it was reconvened, and proposals were finalised, the war ended, making the measures merely academic. The inaction of the United Nations in face of the East Pakistan crisis was widely criticized. The conflict also exposed the delay in decision making that failed to address the underlying issues in time. This habit of United Nations has never changed even today. UN took more than a month to resolve the Israel-Hezbollah crisis and cease-fire was declared on 14th August 2006. This date of 14th August should remind UN to avoid making yet another mistake by neglecting Pakistan. Pakistan is now a most dangerous country on the globe. Pakistan is a threat to the entire humanity not because of its being an Islamic Republic but because of its involvement in organizing international terrorism from its soil. ISI being Pakistan's main brainpower and sole sponsor of terrorist activities around the world, it is equally necessary to take immediate notice of such an organization.

In my petition written in 2001 which was posted on various websites since then, I had suggested that reshaping of the geography of South Asia in order to combat international terrorism had become necessary in the following words:

'*The entire terrorism network has been managed by terrorist forces stationed in Pakistan under the safe umbrella of Government of Pakistan. These terrorist forces have taken the shelter of Islamic identity in order to implement their dangerous designs of dominating South Asia and make it an Islamic territory altogether thereby driving out Christians, Hindus and Sikhs living in India. The ultimate scheme was first made during the lifetime of late General Zia-ul-Haq who can be termed as the main actor towards this direction. The said General Zia-ul-Haq took advantage of the then Afghan-Russian war and made it possible to develop a terrorist network in the region by sponsoring extremist Islamic groups and providing them all necessary military training and ammunition. The atomic program of Pakistan was also part of this endeavor. However, General Zia-ul-Haq died in a military plane crash in 1988 and there was the beginning of a new democratic era in Pakistan. But this democracy was itself fake in the sense that same old faces appeared to rule the country for their own monetary benefits. Consequently, Pakistan became yet another victim of terrorist forces which acted from the strong base of Pakistan Army which has been the main principal of all terrorism in the South Asia. It was Pakistan Army which does not want any peace in the region so as to keep the region under stress in general and to keep India being their hostile neighbor under a constant military threat.*

The coming back of Pakistan Army in power through General Pervez Musharraf from the back doors on October 12, 1999 was yet another attempt to continue with the same old plan of Islamic domination in South Asia as masterminded by late General Zia-ul-Haq. This conspiracy had enjoyed assistance of China as China needed a strong Pakistan to keep an eye on India so that India should not become any problem for China in her traditional desire to win the regional supremacy which may pave way for her becoming another super war.

Pakistan is the central headquarters of all terrorist activities under the authoritative command of Inter-Services Intelligence (ISI) an organ of Pakistan Army who have been sheltering Islamic terrorists organizations in the country through military as well as financial support. Their objective is simple that is to rule the region under an Islamic system of their own brand and elimination of non-Muslim communities and culture. They believe that unless they use power they cannot fulfil their ambitions and as such they have found terrorism as the most convenient method for accomplishment of their political agenda. In order to promote this terrorism through religious recognition and some historic significance with a view to make it attractive for the youngsters, they misinterpreted the concept of Jihad (holy war) and since the Muslim masses living in that region are totally illiterate and ignorant about their own religion, they were misguided by the help of hypocrite Islamic scholars who motivated and induced the foolish young Muslims to fight against non-Muslims. These fools did not even think that if it was the question of Muslim and Non-Muslim, then they should also fight China being totally out of the religious orbit. But, in that case, their brains do not work because it is but China itself which is assisting the Pakistan Army in such activities. Hence, the entire phenomenon is not to propagate the Muslim beliefs but to conquer the whole world through the assistance of China. Pakistan right now is the puppet of China and therefore it has become inevitable to address this issue on top priority.

Chinese experts in connivance with the Pakistan Army have worked very intelligently to use the religion of Islam as a tool very useful to be used for extracting cheap fighting force in the name of holy war. On the other hand, the whole Pakistan Army getting salaries in millions of dollars per annum is not coming forward for this s-called Jihad simply for the reason that they know that it has nothing to do with any Jihad but to implement certain long-term political plans. It is, therefore, very essential to focus from a different angle without wasting any further time on Osama Bin Laden who is nobody but a well-trained puppet of Pakistan Army being used extensively for the purpose of masterminding the terrorist schemes and implementing them through the technical co-operation of Pakistan.

Inter Services Intelligence Agency (ISI) is the real government in Pakistan. In the present situation it is the ISI, which is devising the self-made covert policies for the Government and also ensuring its implementation. It is part of the ISI's well-established policy to organize violent pro-Taliban protest demonstrations against the United States in the provinces of Sindh, Balochistan and NWFP (North West Frontier Province) and keep the province of Punjab away from these demonstrations and strikes. After the terrorist attacks of 11th September 2001, the United States and the international community declared in clear words that we would now see that "who stands with us or against us". The United States and international community assured the Pakistani rulers that if they extend co-operation to United States and international community in the war against terrorism, Pakistan would get the legitimate fruits of such co-operation. After these assurances of the International Community, the ISI conspired to activate the religious and so-called Jihadi groups on their payroll to use the provinces of Sindh, Balochistan and NWFP (North-West Frontier Province) provinces as their battleground against United States and International Community. This conspiracy to use the minority provinces was aimed to give the United States of America and the International Community a completely wrong impression that people living in these provinces are against USA while the real situation is totally different. Pakistan Army through its terrorism network called ISI has made an attempt to tarnish the image of small provinces of present Pakistan on one hand and on the other to deceive USA and the International Community. It is a bitter truth that the province of Punjab is the hub of all the fanatical and so-called Jihadi groups and the Headquarters of all the fanatical and extremists groups are situated in different cities of the province of Punjab like Lahore, Multan, Jhang, Faisalabad and Nankana. The ISI's "game" to deceive the United States and international community would not last long and this act of deception would reach to its logical conclusion. When that happens the world would know who actually benefited by deceiving others and who lost, whereas who was deceived by whom and who was hoodwinked.

It is not understandable as to why the Americans are not addressing the real issue. The real issue is Pakistan itself. In Pakistan, there is no religious disintegration right now. Rather all the religious groups are having mental equation when it is about the religion. There is no conflict among them if it is about Islam. Although they advocate a different Islam which was never the one introduced by Muhammad Bin Abdullah in Mecca some 1500 years ago, yet they are together under the supervision of ISI. ISI has sponsored this new brand of Islam with ulterior motives and to implement its hidden agenda. This new brand of Islam does not enjoy any recognition from the Muslims who really believe in Muhammad. It is indeed unfortunate that Islam has always been victimized throughout by the people who terms themselves as Muslims. Muhammad's Islam was hijacked even in his own lifetime when there were people who disliked Muhammad's relatives and wives. Such miscreants even accused Muhammad's wife Ayesha of adultery. People like Amir Mawiya hated Ali, the nephew of Muhammad so much so that Ali wrote to him several letters condemning Amir Mawiya to be a hypocrite. The revenge came exactly 50 years later when son of Amir Mawiya called

Yazeed killed Hussain brutally who was the grand son of Muhammad and son of Ali at the place called Karbala (Iraq). The shia sect of Islam condemn this brutal murder of Hussain and do not recognize Ami Mawiya as Muslim for this arbitrary act of his son Yazeed. Today, Iran is the shia state while a large number of Shias live in Iraq also. It was one of the evil designs of late General Zia-ul-Haq that he made Pakistan a difficult place for shias and the formation of certain militant religious organizations was yet part of this plan. Today we have yet another Yazeed bin Amir Mawiya called Osama Bin Laden and several followers who have changed the very fabric of Islam in the new century. These are religious demons representing the Satan and not Islam.

It is, therefore, necessary to disintegrate Pakistan if we want to collapse the terrorists' network altogether. Unless we destroy the root cause of the whole terrorism tree, we will not be able to eliminate terrorism from the region which has been transformed into a centralized processing unit working under an integrated system not conveniently accessible unless Pakistan is divided in at least four parts. It is essential to divide the northern part of Pakistan into two countries that is Punjabistan and Pakhtoonistan. The Punjabistan will be on the eastern side and the present province of Punjab can be converted into Punjabistan while the North West Frontier Province (NWFP) having its borders with Afghanistan should be made another country called Pakhtoonistan. The new Pakhtoonistan will be a country loyal to the international comity of nations and shall not harbor any terrorists within its geography. Punjabistan shall not have any access to terrorist camps now being run by Pakistan Army in Afghanistan and NWFP as Pakhtoonistan will be a hurdle between Afghanistan and Punjabistan. The Pakistan Army mainly belongs to Punjab and hence the creation of Punjabistan and Pakhtoonistan will break the integrated network between Afghanistan and ISI (Pakistan Army).

On the southern part of Pakistan, two new countries Sindhudesh and Jinnahpur can be made. The Sindhudesh will comprise of Sindhis living in the province of Sindh while Jinnahpur will be a country to house the urdu speaking immigrants from India who had migrated from India after partition of 1947. The population of urdu speaking community living in Karachi (the main commercial city of Pakistan) is around 15 Million. This new country called Jinnahpur can be a secular state of its own kind. The idea is that some 10 million Christians from India may also voluntarily migrate to Jinnahpur to form a pure secular state in South Asia so as to keep a political balance in the region. In Karachi alone (which will be transformed into a new country called Jinnahpur), we can have as many churches as we want along with awarding rights of preaching Christianity and Islam in parallel terms. There will be no extraordinary religious resistance in Karachi for the sole reason that the new countries

Pakhtoonistan and Punjabistan will have no immediate links with Jinnahpur and as such the terrorist network would not be effective at all. The preaching groups like Tablighi Jamaat (Muslim Preaching Organization based in Raiwind near Lahore-Pakistan) will no more be as effective as now after losing their linkage with their country-wide network. This linkage can only be broken through disintegration of Pakistan. The religious schools called Madressas will no longer be connected with each other. The so-called religious scholars will be confined to their own areas of birth and permanent residence and shall not freely move to other cities in the region presently called Pakistan. Jinnahpur will be a purely secular state with a significant Christian population. We can have permanent airbases of USA and other military set-ups in Jinnahpur to keep a sound military control in the region to safeguard the entire humanity from the threats of terrorism.

The geography of South Asia has to be revised to combat the terrorism and to prevent further loss of lives in the name of Jihad. The region has become very dangerous to spark 3rd world war and if not checked at this hour of need, country like Pakistan, which has attained nuclear technology due to assistance of China, can become dangerous for the whole humanity. Today we have some loyal people in Pakistan Army who would prefer to favor anti-terrorism drive initiated by the Americans. But what about the religious groups within Pakistan Army which are equally responsible in promotion of terrorism in the name of Islamic domination and are still busy to destabilize the international efforts towards the direction of elimination of terrorism altogether. How can such religious groups destroy their own puppet government called Taliban whom they helped right from its inception and are still harboring their leaders and terrorists like Osama Bin Laden. They may come into power and remove General Pervez Musharaf from his present status. What the Americans will do when a more religious-minded foolish army man captures power in Pakistan? Will they think of bringing back of democracy in Pakistan? It will be too late at that time. It is therefore better to act now.

Pakistan should be divided into four parts as immediately as possible under the super-vision of United Nations in the best interest of humanity. This would not be any sort of denying any sovereign country of its right to exist. Pakistan is comprised of five nations and there is no problem in giving these nations their new countries to enable them to have a more realistic identity of their own. This is necessary to eliminate the roots of terrorism completely. This geo-political surgery has become inevitable to save the humanity from the cruel hands of terrorists who will come again to strike and they have no other place to hide and conspire but Pakistan.

I request the entire humanity to join me in this campaign of disintegrating Pakistan in the best interest of the whole humanity. If we break Pakistan today, we are disintegrating the entire terrorist network headquartered in Pakistan. This terrorist network works through a very technical integration in terms of Islamic militant groups, Islamic preaching organizations and Islamic schools called Madressas. A divided Pakistan will destroy the spinal cord of the terrorism and there will be no training camps, no more Osamas and no more threat to humanity.'

Source: **DIVIDE PAKISTAN TO ELIMINATE TERRORISM** Petition
DIVIDE PAKISTAN TO ELIMINATE TERRORISM Petition...
DIVIDE PAKISTAN TO ELIMINATE TERRORISM. View Current Signatures—Sign the Petition
www.petitiononline.com/PAK47/petition.html—*22k*—
www.voiceofthebelievers.com/Activist

Pakistan's disintegration can be argued by certain critics. I, therefore, request these critics to study the disintegration of Yugoslavia in 1945 and Soviet Union in 80s.

On January 31, 1946, the new constitution of Federal People's Republic of Yugoslavia, modeling the Soviet Union, established six Socialist Republics, and two Socialist Autonomous Provinces that were part of SR Serbia. The federal capital was Belgrade. Republics and provinces were:

1. Socialist republic of Bosnia and Herzegovina

2. Socialist republic of Croatia

3. Socialist republic of Macedonia

4. Socialist republic of Montenegro

5. Socialist republic of Serbia, with capital in Belgrade, which also contained:

   5a. Socialist autonomous province ofKosovo

   5b. Socialist autonomous province of Vojvodina

6. Socialist republic of Slovenia

In 1974, the two provinces of Vojvodina and Kosovo as well as the republics of Bosnia & Herzegovina and Montenegro were granted greater autonomy to the point that Albanian and Hungarian became nationally recognised minority languages and the Serbo-Croat of Bosnia and Montenegro altered to a form based on the speech of the local people and not on the standards of Zagreb and Belgrade. Vojvodina and Kosovo form a part of the Republic of Serbia.

If Yugoslavia and Soviet Union were subjected to disintegration for the sake of world peace, why not Pakistan?

REALITY OF 'INTER-SERVICES INTELLIGENCE (ISI)' AND ITS FUNCTIONS

Inter-Services Intelligence (ISI) is a Pakistan-sponsored intelligence agency involved in designing and implementing terrorist activities in South Asia and making future plans for destruction of USA, Israel, and India. The Directorate for Inter-Services Intelligence [ISI] was founded in 1948 by a British army officer, Maj Gen R Cawthome. Field Marshal Ayub Khan, the president of Pakistan in the 1950s, expanded the role of ISI in safeguarding Pakistan's interests, monitoring opposition politicians, and sustaining military rule in Pakistan. This was the beginning of ISI's involvement in terrorist activities with a motive to crush all infidel states in the world and to form a Islamic world order. Former DG of ISI Lt. General Hameed Gul also revealed in a recent TV interview that ISI looks forward to transform the world into an Islamic society from the platform of Pakistan. Hence, Pakistan is being used and shall continue to be used as a platform or launching pad to introduce Wahabi version of Islam which is nothing but cruelty, terrorism, hypocrisy and anarchy.

The ISI is tasked with collection of foreign and domestic intelligence; co-ordination of intelligence functions of the three military services; surveillance over its cadre, foreigners, the media, politically active segments of Pakistani society, diplomats of other countries accredited to Pakistan and Pakistani diplomats serving outside the country; the interception and monitoring of communications; and the conduct of covert offensive operations.

ISI is undoubtedly a state within a state, answerable neither to the leadership of the army, nor to the President or the Prime Minister. The result is there has been no real supervision of the ISI, and corruption, narcotics, and big money have all come into play, further complicating the political scenario. Drug money was used by ISI to finance not only the Afghanistan war, but also the ongoing proxy war against India in Kashmir and Northeast India.

The Joint Chiefs of Staff Committee deals with all problems bearing on the military aspects of state security and is charged with integrating and coordinating the three services. Affiliated with the committee are the offices of the engineer in chief, the director general of medical service, the Director of Inter-Services Public Relations, and the Director of Inter-Services Intelligence.

Staffed by hundreds of civilian and military officers, and thousands of other workers, the agency's headquarters is located in Islamabad. The ISI reportedly has a total of about 10,000 officers and staff members, a number which does not include informants and foreign-based workers and spies disguised as journalists.

ISI is reportedly organized into the following divisions:

- **The Joint Intelligence X (JIX)** which serves as the central secretariat. It coordinates and provides administrative support to the other ISI wings and field organisations. It also prepares intelligence estimates and threat assessments

- **The Joint Intelligence Bureau (JIB)**, responsible for political intelligence and therefore considered as most powerful unit within ISI. The JIB consists of three subsections, with one subsection devoted to operations against USA's army personnel in Afghanistan (operational since 2002) apart from other two subsections devoted to plans against India and Iran

- **The Joint Counter Intelligence Bureau (JCIB)** is responsible for field surveillance of Pakistani diplomats stationed abroad, as well as for conducting intelligence operations in the Middle East, South Asia, China, Afghanistan and the Muslim republics of the former Soviet Union

- **The Joint Drug Control and Surveillance Unit (JDCSU)** which is responsible to monitor poppy cultivation in different parts of Pakistan and Afghanistan undertaken under the supervision of Pakistan Government for raising funds for further expansion of military strength and funding of Jihadi groups in Afghanistan and Kashmir

- **The Joint Intelligence/North (JIN)** is responsible for Jammu and Kashmir and Waziristan operations, including infiltration, exfilteration, propaganda and other clandestine operations

- **The Joint Intelligence Miscellaneous (JIM)** conducts espionage in foreign countries, including offensive intelligence operations

- **The Joint Signal Intelligence Bureau (JSIB)**, which includes Deputy Directors for Wireless, Monitoring and Photos, operates a chain of signals intelligence collection stations along the border with India, Iran and Afghanistan and provide communication support to militants operating in Kashmir and at Pak-Afghan border

- **The Joint Intelligence Technical (JIT)** which deals with certain technical matters

- **The Joint Intelligence Internet (Internet Section)** which deals with information obtained from internet sites about Pakistan, its government, its army and Pakistan's involvement in terrorist activities

In addition to these main elements, ISI also includes a separate explosives section and a chemical warfare section. Published reports provide contradictory indications as to the relative size of these organizational elements, suggesting that either JIX is the largest, or that the Joint Intelligence Bureau is the largest with some sixty percent of the total staff.

The Directorate for Inter-Services Intelligence is of particular importance at the joint services level. The directorate's importance derives from the fact that the agency is charged with managing covert operations outside of Pakistan. The ISI supplies weapons, training, advice and planning assistance to terrorists in Kashmir and the the Northeast frontier areas of India.

The ISI has been deeply involved in domestic politics and, has kept track of the incumbent regime's opponents. Prior to the imposition of Martial Law in 1958, ISI reported to the Commander-in-Chief of the Army (C-in-C). When martial Law was promulgated in 1958 all the intelligence agencies fell under the direct control of the President and Chief Martial Law Administrator, and the three intelligence agencies began competing to demonstrate their loyalty to Ayub Khan and his government.

The ISI became even more deeply involved in domestic politics under General Yahya Khan, notably in East Pakistan, where operations were mounted to ensure that no political party should get an overall majority in the general election. Mr. Bhutto, former Prime Minister of Pakistan promoted General Zia-Ul-Haq in part because the Director of ISI, General Gulam Jilani Khan, was actively promoting him. General Zia, in return, retained General Jilani as head of ISI after his scheduled retirement. The ISI became much more effective under the leadership of Hameed Gul. The 1990 elections were rigged under the auspices of ISI in order to prevent Benazir Bhutto from becoming Pakistan's Prime Minister again for the sole reason that she belonged to SINDH. The Islami Jamhoori Ittehad [IJI] party was a conglomerate formed of nine mainly rightist parties by the ISI under Lt General Hameed Gul to ensure the defeat of Bhutto's Pakistan People's Party (PPP) in the polls.

The Soviet invasion of Afghanistan made Pakistan a country of paramount geostrategic importance. In a matter of days, the United States declared Pakistan a "frontline state" against Soviet aggression and offered to reopen aid and military assistance deliveries. Pakistan's top national security agency, the Army's Directorate for Inter-Services Intelligence, monitored the activities of and provided advice and support to the mujahidin, and commandos from the Army's Special Services Group helped guide the operations inside Afghanistan. The ISI trained about 90,000 Afghan Fighters between 1983 to 1997 and dispatched them to Afghanistan. This training also included an organized 'brain-washing' conducted by Tablighi Jamat which represents ISI's newly formed Religious Cult Group for providing assistance in the field of brain-washing of prospective 'Fighters' and 'Suicide Bombers' Pakistan paid a price for its activities, as Afghan and Soviet forces conducted raids against mujahidin bases inside Pakistan.

The ISI continued to actively participate in Afghan Civil War, supporting the Taliban in their fight against the then Rabbani government. Backing of the Taliban officially ended after the terrorist attacks of September 11, 2001 since the Fascist military ruler General Pervez Musharraf decided to save Pakistan's soil from any bloodshed. However, General Pervez Musharraf ordered ISI to continue to aid Taliban fighters and sending reinforcement consistently.

ISI has also been engaged in covertly supporting the Kashmiri Mujahideen in their fight against the Indian authorities in Kashmir. Famous "Operation Tupac" was the designation of the three part action plan for the capture of Kashmir through proxy warfare, initiated by President Zia Ul Haq in 1988 after the failure of "Operation Gibraltar." According to a report compiled by the Joint Intelligence Committee (JIC) of India in 1995, ISI spent about $4 Million per month to sponsor its activities in Jammu and Kashmir. Although all groups reportedly received arms and training from Pakistan, the pro-Pakistani groups were reputed to be favored by the ISI. As of May 1996, at least six major militant organizations, and several smaller ones, operated in Kashmir. Their forces were variously estimated at between 5,000 and 10,000 armed men.

The oldest and most widely known militant organization, the Jammu and Kashmir Liberation Front (JKLF), spearheaded the movement for an Independent Kashmir. This group declared a cease-fire in 1994. The most powerful of the pro-Pakistani groups is the Hezb-ul-Mujahedin. The other major groups are Harakat-ul Ansar, a group which has a large number of non-Kashmiris in it, Al Umar, Al Barq, Jaish-e-Mohammad, and Lashkar-e Taiba, which is also made up largely of fighters from Afghanistan and Pakistan trained and brain-washed under the auspices of ISI and Tablighi Jamat respectively. Many of these militants were trained in Afghanistan and certain parts of NWFP. Since the defeat of the Taliban, militant training camps have moved to Pakistani Kashmir and hilly tracks in Punjab.

ISI has also been operating training camps near the border of Bangladesh where members of separatist groups of the northeastern states, known as the "United Liberation Front Of Seven Sisters" [ULFOSS] are trained with military equipment and terrorist activities. These groups include the National Security Council of Nagaland [NSCN], People's Liberation Army [PLA], United Liberation Front of Assam [ULFA], and North East Students Organization [NESO].

Pakistan's hypocrite and Fascist military leader, General Pervez Musharraf, has his own interaction with ISI. Since September 11th 2001, Islamic fundamentalists have been purged from leadership positions on the interference of USA. The then-ISI head Lieutenant General Mahmood Ahmed was replaced in October 2001 by Lieutenant General Ehsanul Haq in line with this interference. General Pervez Musharaff actually hid the main terrorist activities of ISI by giving a soft satisfaction to USA by such action. On the contrary, Pervez Musharraf never stopped terrorist activities of ISI at any stage. Similarly, additional reforms of the ISI have been made. Most notable was the decision to disband the Kashmir and Afghanistan units officially. However, they were restructured in a different form since both these groups have promoted Islamic fundamentalist militancy throughout South Asia. This restructuring is not in the knowledge of USA or foreign intelligence agencies. As far as I know, Raiwind-Lahore is the newest headquarter of ISI's religious units engaged in making, organizing and controlling evil plans of terrorism in the disguise of Islamic preaching group called Tablighi Jamat.

Inter-Services Intelligence (ISI) has done what coward Pakistan Army could dream of. It has captured the vitals of the nation, its tentacles are spread across every nook and cranny-from Gujarat (India) to Assam (India) from Kashmir to Kerala (India). Mumbai Bombings are also a display of ground realities about the existence of ISI's terrorist networks operating at different locations in South Asia. It can trigger blasts in remote places, fuel communal riots in peaceful cities and blow up railway stations anywhere it wishes to. It can spread terror wherever, whenever. Its control is full and final. There is not a city in South Asia which doesn't have either an active or a sleeping agent of the ISI. This agent can be an 'Imam' leading prayers in a nearby mosque or a friend next door or a cooperative neighbour or the local tailor or a preaching group (Tablighi Jamat) staying in the local mosque for the purpose of preaching Islam. They have been brainwashed or inculcated into the fold by the ISI either by financial allurement or in the name of religion. Whatever might be the provocation, the ISI agents are motivated enough to carry out the orders of their masters in Islamabad. The ISI has taken more than 28 years to implement its plan of action. After the 1971 bifurcation of erstwhile Pakistan into two nations, the ISI, which works under the overall control of the Pak Army, has been working with the sole objective of avenging the defeat and crush India. The plan was conceived by President Ziaul-Haq and was called Operation Topac. The objectives of Operation Topac were;

a.   to disintegrate India;

b.   to utilise the spy network to act as an instrument of sabotage;

c.   to exploit porous borders with Nepal and Bangladesh to set up bases and conduct operations.

A close look at the ISI structure as it exists in Pakistan will reveal the extent of Islamabad's nefarious designs. The ISI has been concentrating on India's Punjab, especially after Bhindaranwale inspired terrorism was quashed by KPS Gill and his band of supercops. Since then, the ISI has been promoting various terrorist groups like the International Sikh Youth Federation led by Lakhbir Singh Rode, Khalistan Commando Force, Babbar Khalsa International and Khalistan Liberation Force of Pritam Singh Sekhon. The ISI has been working in the North-East and Southern parts of India. Its links with North-East insurgents are well exposed to the international community. It has not only been funding some out of the militant outfits but also been providing them with arms and ammunition and training facilities in neighbouring Nepal. The ISI's hand in the Mumbai and

Coimbatore blasts has proved that it has been working quietly in spreading a terror network all over South Asia. ISI's agents are moving around freely, setting up bombs and creating communal rifts with impunity within India. Is ISI's existence not dangerous for the security of a great country like India which has entered 21st century with lots of potentials and prospective ability to become an economic power in another 10–15 years. If this is certain that ISI is dangerous, why there is delay in destructing it through disintegration of Pakistan. Only Pakistan's division can crush the existence of ISI's network. USA and UK with due cooperation of European Union, India and Iran should decide now if they want to save 21st century from a possible nuclear disaster which can be caused by the fanatic soldiers of Islam under the banner of Wahabi Islam (sponsored by Saudi Kingdom) being nourished by ISI and Tablighi Jamat.

Reflections of ISI can be found in the following news reports:

February 2005: A federal jury in Manhattan convicted defense lawyer Lynne F. Stewart, 65, of conspiring to provide support to terrorism by smuggling messages out of jail from her convicted terrorist client Sheikh `Umar Abd Al-Rahman and making them known to his followers in Egypt. The sheikh is serving a life sentence for inspiring a foiled 1993 plot to bomb the United Nations, the Lincoln and Holland Tunnels, and other New York landmarks. Codefendant Ahmed Abdel Sattar, 45, was convicted of conspiring to kill and kidnap in a foreign country and of soliciting violence for an October 2000 fatwa that he helped compose that called on Muslims around the world "to fight the Jews and kill them wherever they are." Codefendant Mohamed Yousry, 48, was convicted of three counts of terrorism and conspiracy. Ms. Stewart was sentenced in July 2005. *(Comment: This Fatwa is considered as an authoritative religious decree by Pakistan's Tablighi Jamat which also confirms that such Fatwas are valid and enforceable. Tablighi Jamat is working closely with ISI)*

February 2005: In federal district court in Jackson, Mississippi, two New Orleans men, Cedric Carpenter and Lamont Ranson, pleaded guilty to their involvement in a conspiracy to sell false identity documents to purported members of the Philippines-based terrorist group Abu Sayyaf, designated by the U.S. as a foreign terrorist organization. As part of the guilty plea, both defendants admitted to conspiring to provide material support to a foreign terrorist organization. The men were arrested at their homes in New Orleans in August 2004 after an elaborate federal sting operation. *(Comment: These Filipinos were members of Tablighi*

Jamat in Philippines and had also spent time in Tablighi Jamat's headquarters in Manila)

March 2005: A criminal complaint issued in December 2004 and unsealed in March 2005 charges former Detroit and Washington, D.C., public schools official Kifah Wael Jayyousi, 43, and Kassem Daher, formerly of Broward County, Florida, of conspiring to provide material support and resources for terrorism, and with conspiracy to kill, kidnap, maim, or injure people or damage property in a foreign country. The two allegedly raised money and recruited Islamic extremists to fight in Bosnia, Kosovo, Chechnya, and Somalia. Jordanian national and naturalized American citizen Jayyousi was arrested at the Detroit Metro Airport after arriving from Amsterdam. Daher is a fugitive living in Lebanon. *(Comment: Kassem Daher was closely involved in activities of Tablighi Jamat in USA)*

April 2005: Kifah Wael Jayyousi, an adjunct engineering professor at Wayne State University in Detroit who previously served as the chief facilities director for public schools in Washington, D.C., from 1999 to 2001, was arrested by U.S. customs agents on March 27 at Detroit Metro Airport after arriving from Qatar where he had been visiting his father. Jayyousi, a Jordanian-born U.S. citizen who had been living in Qatar since 2003, and two associates were described by federal prosecutor Russell Killinger as "primary participants in a triangulated North American support cell." *(Comment: Jayyousi was a regular visitor to various preaching sessions organized by Tablighi Jamat in Jordan)*

April 2005: Former British clothing merchant Hemant Lakhani, 69, was convicted in Newark, New Jersey, of trying to sell shoulder-launched missiles to what he believed was a terrorist group planning to shoot down airliners. Arrested in 2003 after a federal sting operation, Lakhani was convicted of attempting to provide material support to terrorists and money laundering. *(Comment: Lakhani was also sympathiser of Tablighi Jamat)*

April 2005: British student pilot Zayead Christopher Hajaig, a.k.a. Barry John Felton, 35, was indicted by a federal grand jury on charges of being an illegal alien in possession of weapons. Hajaig attended the same flight school in Georgia at which two of the September 11 hijackers briefly trained. A terrorism alert was issued after he allegedly tried to have his pilot rating upgraded to fly commercial aircraft, despite not being qualified. Hajaig fled to Britain, where he was arrested.

May 2005: A court in Portland, Oregon, sentenced Palestinian Ali Khalid Steitiye, 42, to five years in prison for carrying a machine gun during target practice alongside members of an Oregon terror cell. Steitiye, who will be deported following completion of his sentence, was present when members of the so-called "Portland Seven" terror cell were engaged in firearms training. Cell members were accused of conspiring to travel to Afghanistan to help the Taliban fight the U.S. military; six are serving prison terms while the seventh, Habis Abdulla al Saoub, was reported killed in an October 2003 shootout in Pakistan.

May 2005: Federal authorities arrested two former officers of an Islamic charity—Emadeddin Z. Muntasser, 40, the former president of the Boston-based charity Care International, and Muhamed Mubayyid, 40, the group's former treasurer, on charges of lying to authorities investigating the charity's alleged ties to terrorist organizations and of conspiring to defraud the U.S. According to the indictment, Care International was the Boston branch of the Brooklyn-based Al-Kifah Refugee Center, and was involved in supporting jihad activities.

June-July 2005: A federal grand jury in Sacramento, California, indicted Umer Hayat, 47, and his son Hamid Hayat, 22, on three counts of making false statements to the FBI related to international and domestic terrorism. According to the indictment, the defendants lied about their attending jihadist terrorist training camps in Pakistan. The Hayats have not been charged with any terrorist-related activity but papers filed in federal court said Hamid Hayat admitted to interrogators that he attended an Al Qa`ida training camp in Pakistan. Along with the Hayats, three Pakistanis from Lodi-Muslim leader Muhammed Adil Khan, 47, his son, Mohammad Hassan Adil, 19, and Lodi mosque imam Shabbir Ahmed, 42-were arrested on alleged immigration violations. In July 2005, the Khans agreed to return to Pakistan.
(Comments: These Khans are also sympathisers of Tablighi Jamat)

July 2005: Pakistan's president, Gen. Pervez Musharraf, said Monday that al-Qaeda was too weak to organize terrorist attacks from his country. But U.S. Attorney General Alberto Gonzales has said the attacks in Egypt and London appear to be the work of al-Qaeda. And in London, Police Commissioner Ian Blair said he believes al-Qaeda-linked terrorists were involved in both the deadly July 7 and the failed July 21 attacks on the London Underground.

Musharraf did acknowledge that small groups of al-Qaeda militants might still be hiding in Pakistan's North and South Waziristan tribal regions, where Pakistani security forces have carried out several operations. al-Qaeda leader Osama bin Laden is believed to be in that area (source: USATODAY 25th July 2005)

July 2005: On Monday, Egyptian police circulated photographs of the five Pakistanis who have been missing since several days before Saturday's attacks at checkpoints in and around the southern city of Sharm el-Sheik (Egypt). Investigators were looking into whether the men had any involvement in Saturday's attack. (source: USATODAY 25th July 2005)

July 2005: FBI and Homeland Security agents raided the Northern Virginia office of the Saudi-based charity Muslim World League (MWL) and arrested Saudi citizen and organization employee Abdullah Alnoshan, 44, on charges of immigration fraud. Also charged in the case was Sudanese citizen Khalid Fadlalla, who worked in the MWL New York office. The organization has been under U.S. government scrutiny for possible links to Osama bin Ladin.

September 15, 2004: The Spanish police arrested 10 Pakistanis suspected of involvement in Islamic extremism during an operation in the northeastern region of Catalonia, reported AFP. Judicial sources in Madrid said the suspects were arrested 'for Islamic terrorism' and said all were of Pakistani origin. A police spokesperson said the Pakistani suspects "could have financed radical organisations outside Spain's borders." Five of the Pakistanis were detained in the northern Barcelona district of Trinitat Vella and five more in the central 'Barrio chino' or Chinese district, where there is a concentration of Pakistanis. Foreign Office spokesperson Masood Khan said in Islamabad that those arrested by the Spanish police also included some Pakistani citizens.

September 13, 2004: Cambodian police arrested four men believed to be of Pakistani origin over the weekend in connection with terrorist activities, a Government spokesman confirmed on September 13. Government spokesperson Khieu Kanharith told Deutsche Presse-Agentur (DPA) that Cambodian police had arrested four men, but refused to confirm Radio Free Asia reports that they were of Pakistani origin.

September 9, 2004: At least 50 terrorists, including some Chechens, Uzbeks and Arabs, are reported to have been killed and 120 others were wounded during an aerial raid on their training camp at Bad Awaz Garang in the Kaikhel area of South Waziristan.

September 7, 2004: An Al Qaeda-linked Saudi terrorist, identified as Abdullah, is arrested from a house at Shakas village in the Jamrud district, about 25 kilometers west of Peshawar. According to Dawn, he had lived in the area for many years and that he had been arrested once before, in the late 1990s.

September 1, 2004: The security agencies are reported to have arrested two foreigners, including a man believed to be a senior Al Qaeda operative, during a raid in Quetta, capital of Balochistan province, said official sources. The suspects, an Egyptian identified as Sharif Al Misri and Saudi national Abdul Hakeem, were arrested on August 29 from the Ghausabad area of Quetta.

August 30, 2004: Two Arabs were reportedly arrested from the Hayatabad area in Peshawar on suspicion of being Al Qaeda operatives.

August 28, 2004: Daily Times reported that a Pakistani national and a US citizen were arrested over an alleged plot to blow up a subway station in New York. City police commissioner Raymond Kelly said that "it is clear they had the intention to cause damage and kill people". But he said there was no immediate evidence that they were connected to Al Qaeda or any international terrorist groups.

August 26, 2004: Sajjad Nasser, a Pakistani national accused of attending a terrorist training camp, is deported from the United States to Pakistan. Nasser was deported under a section of the Patriot Act that expands the legal definitions of terrorist organizations and acts, said Corina Almeida, chief counsel for US Immigration and Customs Enforcement. Nasser was arrested in March 2003 on charges of conspiring to harbour an illegal resident. Immigration authorities accused him of attending a training camp run by the Pakistan-based Jaish-e-Mohammed.

August 24, 2004: Four Uzbek nationals were arrested for alleged terrorist links during a raid in South Waziristan, said Interior Minister Faisal Saleh Hayyat.

August 23, 2004: Security forces are reported to have killed four Uzbek terrorists during an encounter in the Miranshah area of North Waziristan. Separately, seven Afghan nationals were arrested for their alleged links to the Al Qaeda in Malakwal on the same day.

August 22, 2004: President Pervez Musharraf discloses that a Libyan Al Qaeda suspect masterminded the two assassination attempts on him during December

2003. He is "the mastermind behind the two plots," Gen. Musharraf said this in an interview to the Time magazine, to be published on Aug 30.

August 20, 2004: An Uzbek terrorist and a member of the Zalikhel sub-tribe were reportedly killed during the ongoing clashes between terrorists and troops in the Santoi and Mantoi mountains of South Waziristan.

August 19, 2004: Two foreign nationals allegedly linked to the Al Qaeda were arrested after a brief encounter with the security force personnel in the Hayatabad township of Peshawar. While one of the suspects was identified as Mohammad Fauzi, an Algerian national, the other is reportedly an Iraqi national.

August 17, 2004: Security agencies in Lahore have reportedly arrested two more Al Qaeda suspects for their alleged involvement in a suicide attack on Finance Minister Shaukat Aziz. Muhammad Shafiq is suspected to be Taliban chief Mulla Mohammed Omar's close aide while Abu Hamza is an Al Qaeda operative from Myanmar.

August 11, 2004: Four Turkish nationals are reported to have been arrested from Lahore over the weekend for suspected links to the Al Qaeda. While their identities were not officially disclosed, The Nation reported that two of them were 'diehard' operatives of Al Qaeda and fought with the Taliban against US-led coalition forces in Afghanistan. A Pakistani man, arrested from Long Island in New York, has reportedly admitted to smuggling money, night vision goggles and other military gear to a senior Al Qaeda leader in Pakistan near the Pakistan-Afghanistan border, a report in the New York Times said on August 11. Mohammed Junaid Babar allegedly made the confessions to the Federal District Court in Manhattan on June 3, 2004. He pleaded guilty to five counts of conspiring to provide material support to terrorists, according to a transcript of the court proceedings made public on August 10, the report said.

August 9, 2004: Two top Al Qaeda suspects have reportedly been arrested from Karachi and Peshawar on August 9. Mohsin, a Pakistani national who is allegedly linked to the assassination attempts on President Pervez Musharraf, was arrested from Karachi, an unnamed official was quoted as saying in an AFP report. The Uzbek national, identified as Mansoor, was arrested in Peshawar. Security agencies in Lahore are reported to have arrested three foreigners for their alleged links to the Al Qaeda. According to Dawn (Pakistani newspaper), they were arrested during separate raids at a seminary and a rented house in the city. Two of the foreigners are said to be of Turkish origin and the third from an unnamed African country. However, Lahore police chief Tariq Saleem said "Neither any such raid nor is any arrest in our knowledge."

August 8, 2004: According to Daily Times, a senior Al Qaeda operative, Qari Saifullah Akhtar, leader of Harkat-ul-Jehadi-e-Islami (HuJI), has been arrested in Dubai and handed over to Islamabad. Qari was linked to two assassination attempts on President Pervez Musharraf and has been described by one source as "an operational head of al-Qaeda in Pakistan". He was reportedly with Osama bin Laden and Taliban leader Mullah Muhammad Omar in Afghanistan at the time of the US-led war against the Taliban late in 2001 and fled first to Saudi Arabia and subsequently to United Arab Emirates.

August 5, 2004: Interior Minister Faisal Saleh Hayat said in Islamabad that security agencies have arrested 20 suspected terrorists, including Al Qaeda operatives, during the last three weeks. While indicating that some high-value Al Qaeda targets were among those detained, he refused to disclose the identities of these persons.

August 3, 2004: Interior Minister Faisal Saleh Hayat disclosed in Islamabad that two more "high value" Al Qaeda terrorists of African origin were arrested from Punjab. "The head money on these terrorists was also in millions of dollars," he said while addressing a press conference. He also said that the latest arrests were based on information secured from the interrogation of Tanzanian Al Qaeda operative Ahmed Khalfan Ghailani, arrested earlier from Gujarat. According to Daily Times, a police constable in Punjab Chief Minister Choudhury Pervaiz Elahi's security squad has been arrested for allegedly passing on information to Al Qaeda and other terrorist outfits on the movement of important persons.

July 31, 2004: A group claiming to be linked to the Al Qaeda network said that it had tried to assassinate Pakistan's Prime Minister-designate Shaukat Aziz and warned of more attacks against 'pro-US' officials. The Islambouli Brigades did not name Shaukat Aziz in the statement posted on an Islamist website, but said it had targeted one of the men of the "American infidel in Pakistan". Lt Khaled Islambouli was the leader of the group of soldiers, who assassinated Egyptian President Anwar Sadat during a military parade in Cairo in 1981.

July 29, 2004: Pakistan disclosed that it had arrested a senior Al Qaeda terrorist wanted for the 1998 bombings of US embassies in Kenya and Tanzania that killed more than 200 people. Interior Minister Faisal Saleh Hayat identified the man as Ahmed Khalfan Ghailani and said he was a Tanzanian national carrying a head money of $25 million. The Minister stated Ghailani was one of the 12 persons arrested on July 27 when security forces raided a suspected terrorist hideout in the city of Gujarat, about 175 km southeast of the capital Islamabad.

July 25, 2004: Security forces arrested 13 suspected terrorists, including four foreigners and some members of their families, from a house in Gujrat after a 14-hour gunfight that left at least one police personnel wounded. However, there was no official confirmation on the nationalities of the foreigners and if the arrested men belonged to the Al Qaeda network. "Yes, (I can only confirm that) they are terrorists," Punjab Law Minister Muhammad Basharat Raja told Dawn. Referring to their nationalities, he said: "At this moment I can only say that they are foreigners."

July 16, 2004: At least twenty-four Al Qaeda-trained terrorists are still hiding in Karachi, said a top police official, Tariq Jamil, on July 16. They plot attacks while subsidiary cells provide cover in Karachi city, Jamil was quoted as saying in Daily Times, adding that the 24 were the top of a three-tier operational hierarchy. "The second tier provides logistic support and pinpoints potential targets while the third tier is made up of extremely motivated executioners," he said. The official also said the cells operated in small groups and had no central command structure. Security agencies are reportedly unable to ascertain the strength of the second and third tiers.

July 12, 2004: The Afghan President Hamid Karzai said in an interview that terrorists trained in Pakistan were crossing over into his country, adding that his regime was raising this issue with Islamabad on a "daily basis". Karzai told New York Times that he was concerned about the training in Pakistan of terrorists, who then cross over and carry out attacks in Afghanistan.

July 9, 2004: Cyprus is reported to have deported ten Pakistanis for suspected terrorist links. According to Daily Times, ten Pakistani students were deported after being detained by Cyprus police on suspicion of belonging to the Al Qaeda network. One of the suspects, reportedly trained in avionic engineering, had arrived in Cyprus to pursue a course in Hotel Management. "I can't tell you whether they are members of al-Qaeda, we are not sure of that, but it is certain that they fit the profile of terror suspects," an unnamed Cypriot security source told Reuters. The men, who were enrolled at a private Cypriot college in the holiday resort of Larnaca, were arrested on July 7.

July 1, 2004: An Anti Terrorism Court (ATC) in Karachi on July 1 indicted nine activists of the proscribed Harkat-ul-Mujahideen Al-alami (HuMA) for their involvement in the Macedonian consulate bomb blast case. According to prosecution, the accused killed three persons on December 5, 2002, in premises of the Macedonian consulate in Karachi and later blasted the office with explosives. The Macedonian police on May 1, 2004, had acknowledged that the killing of Pakistanis was staged to win United States' support and that the victims were innocent illegal immigrants.

June 30, 2004: According to Daily Times, the Special Investigation Group (SIG) of the police in Islamabad conducted a raid on a house at Mullaha Rajagan on June 30 and arrested three Iraqi nationals and later recovered some weapons, explosive material and building maps. SIG sources were quoted as saying that certain Iraqi nationals had been planning terrorist activities in Pakistan.

June 29,2004: Taliban-led terrorists are still launching operations against American and other forces from safe havens in Pakistan, said US Ambassador to Afghanistan, Zalmay Khalilzad. While stating that a Pakistani military operation in South Waziristan during this month in which at least 100 foreign terrorists and allied tribesmen were killed "really has disrupted" Al Qaeda and Taliban operatives there, he added there were other areas of Pakistan from which Taliban crossed into Afghanistan. "In that regard, there hasn't been any change. They've dealt with part of the problem, but the problem is obviously larger than that," said the Ambassador.

June 27, 2004: According to Daily Times, security forces in South Waziristan arrested an important Al Qaeda 'commander' and his two associates. Muhammad Nazir and his two aides were arrested at Zalai check-post when they were coming from Angoor Ada to Wana.

June 25, 2004: Security agencies in the North West Frontier Province (NWFP) are reported to have arrested a Saudi national and a Pakistani in Chitral, some 230 kilometers north of Peshawar, for suspected terrorist links. The arrested Saudi national, identified as Abdur Rehman, according to Daily Times, has not yet been confirmed as an Al Qaeda operative. The two were arrested from the Bamborete area in Kalash, close to the Afghan border.

June 24, 2004: According to The News, two suspected Al Qaeda operatives, identified as Abdur Rahman alias Abu Obaida and Suleman Tahir, were arrested in Chitral.

June 16, 2004: A US court sentences three persons for conspiring to aid the Lashkar-e-Toiba. Federal Judge Leonie M Brinkema imposed life imprisonment on Masood Khan, an 85-year term on Seifullah Chapman and a 97-month sentence for Abdur Raheem. All three were members of the 'Virginia jihad network'. Judge Brinkema said she was bound by federal sentencing guidelines that imposed mandatory multi-year terms on Chapman and Khan for weapons counts, but she found them "appalling" and urged the prosecutor to request reductions. US Attorney Paul J McNulty, in a statement, said the sentences "are appropriate and reflect the seriousness of the offences." The 11 defendants in the case, most of them reportedly hailing from the Washington suburbs, were indicted in June 2003 on weapons counts and charges of training with the LeT. Khan and another defendant were also charged with conspiring to provide material support to the Al Qaeda and Taliban.

June 15, 2004: According to The News, security forces' killed a suspected Chechen terrorist during an encounter at Jandola check post in South Waziristan. The Chechen was killed and four persons were arrested after an encounter that ensued after troops checked them at Jandola post. Muhamad Syaifudin, an Indonesian student charged with involvement in terrorist activity, claimed on June 15 that he met Osama bin Laden in Karachi before the September 11 attacks, reported The News. Syaifudin was one of the six students deported from Pakistan in December 2003 due to their alleged links with the South-East Asian terrorist group Jemaah Islamiah. "I and my friends had a meeting with Osama bin Laden at Al Farouq mosque in Karachi. The meeting was before the September 11 incident," Syaifudin told reporters before the start of his trial at the Central Jakarta District court.

June 13, 2004: According to Interior Minister Faisal Saleh Hayat, security forces have arrested a nephew of a top Al Qaeda operative and several other foreigners blamed for a series of attacks including the June 10-assassination attempt on the Karachi Corps Commander. They were arrested over the weekend during separate raids in Karachi, said Faisal, adding "They have confessed to a key role in the attack. They have a direct link to al-Qaeda." The Al Qaeda operative, identified as Musabir Urumchi, is reported to be the nephew of Khalid Sheikh Mohammad and had a $1 million reward on his head, said the Minister.

June 12; 2004: The Hindu reports that Lashkar-e-Toiba has set up a full-blown unit in Pakistan for suicide squad operations against Western forces in Iraq. Up to 2,000 men, mainly between the ages of 18 and 25, are believed to have signed up for the armed operations in Iraq. Most Lashkar suicide squad volunteers come from the ranks of seminary students at Muridke in the Pakistani province of Punjab, which is the LeT's overground political patron organisation, the Jamaat-ud-Dawa's main centre. However, some have also been raised from the Binori Town seminary in Karachi, which used to be run by the fundamentalist cleric, Mufti Nizamuddin Shamzai, until he was assassinated.

June 6, 2004: Security forces are reported to have arrested a Russian national from a tribal region, bordering Afghanistan, for his alleged links to the Al Qaeda. The 23-year-old Caucasian, who claimed to hail from a village near Moscow, was arrested at a military checkpoint outside Miranshah. According to The News, he was carrying a fake Pakistani identification card and during interrogation said that he had lived in the tribal region for the past four years.

June 3, 2004: A suspected Uzbek operative of the Al Qaeda and a soldier of Shawal Scouts were killed in a suspected suicide attack, while two soldiers sustained injuries at a check-post in the North Waziristan agency, close to the Afghanistan border.

May 28,2004: A Sri Lankan businessman accused of brokering clandestine deals in nuclear technology was reportedly arrested in Malaysia. Buhary Syed Abu Tahir, who allegedly worked with Pakistani nuclear scientist Abdul Qadeer Khan to sell nuclear secrets to "rogue states", was detained for threatening Malaysia's national security, unnamed officials told The Associated Press. Some terrorists from the Chinese province of Xinjiang are hiding in Lahore and Rawalpindi, Chinese Deputy Director of Public Security, Ma Mingyue, said in Urumqi on May 28. Talking to a group of visiting journalists from Pakistan, Mingyue claimed that members of the East Turkestan Islamic Movement (ETIM) have mixed up with the Chinese community in the two Pakistani cities, according to Daily Times.

May 27, 2004: According to Daily Times, the US-educated Pakistani woman who is among seven "dangerous" Al Qaeda suspects identified on May 26 by the Federal Bureau of Investigation (FBI) was already in the custody of US intelligence agencies for the last one year. Aafia Siddiqui, reportedly an award-winning Massachusetts Institute of Technology (MIT) student, according to intelligence sources had come to Pakistan in January 2003 and stayed with her friend in Islamabad for a few days and later went to Karachi to see her mother. Immediately after landing at Karachi airport she was detained by intelligence personnel and later handed over to the FBI.

May 26, 2004: A Pakistani woman with a doctorate in neurological science is reportedly among the seven "dangerous" Al Qaeda suspects identified by the Federal Bureau of Investigation (FBI) as planners of new terrorist attacks on the United States. Like the other suspects, the 32-year old Aafia Siddiqui, once an award-winning Massachusetts Institute of Technology (MIT) student, has the ability to "undertake planning, facilitation and attack against the United States whether it be within the United States itself or overseas," FBI director Robert Mueller told a news conference in Washington. She is the only woman among the seven named on May 26 and whose photographs were posted on the FBI website, according to AFP. May 25:

Said Tayeb Jawad, Afghan Ambassador to the United States, reportedly said in Washington that the search for Osama bin Laden should be centred in Karachi or Quetta as the chances of his being found in an isolated area were negligible. May 19:

Security agencies in Peshawar are reported to have arrested five Al Qaeda suspects who had allegedly escaped during the Pakistan Army operation in the South Waziristan tribal area. According to Dawn, two Arab nationals, two ethnic Uzbeks and an Afghan were arrested during a raid in the Sultan Colony area.

May 18, 2004: Authorities in NWFP, according to The News, are pursuing the widow of an Uzbek Islamist terrorist after an intelligence report suggested that she was training women suicide bombers. The intelligence report indicated that Aziza, widow of Obaidullah, who was a member of the Islamic Movement of Uzbekistan, would launch attacks in Pakistan in May.

May 11, 2004: In a video posted on an Islamist militant website showing the beheading of an American civilian in Iraq, an Al Qaeda-affiliated group said it is 'ready to take on Pakistani soldiers on the borders with Afghanistan', according to reports in The Associated Press. In the video, titled 'Abu Musab al-Zarqawi shown slaughtering an American', a masked man reads a statement with a message for President Pervez Musharraf. "Another message to the agent traitor Pervez Musharraf, we tell you that we are eager to meet your soldiers. By God, we seek them before the Americans and we will avenge the blood of our brothers in Wana and others," the masked man said.

May 4, 2004: According to Dawn (Pakistan newspaper), a group of alleged terrorists arrested in Turkey on suspicion of planning an attack on a North Atlantic Treaty Organization (NATO) meeting were trained in Pakistan and were planning to carry out a suicide mission against US President George W. Bush. Turkish press reports said that the suspects were allegedly in possession of Turkish-subtitled video cassettes attributed to Osama bin Laden calling for a Jehad against America. They were allegedly planning to bomb the NATO Summit scheduled for June 28 and 29 in Istanbul where Bush and other world leaders will attend, according to police sources quoted by the papers. The suspects were arrested in the northwestern city of Bursa, though no dates were disclosed. The Hurriyet and Vatan newspapers said that several suspects underwent physical and psychological training in Pakistan to prepare them to carry out a suicide attack.

April 29, 2004: Uzbekistan President Islam Karimov said in Tashkent that terrorists responsible for the coordinated series of attacks during March 2004 that killed at least 47 people were based in Pakistan along that country's border with Afghanistan. "The main base where the terrorists found refuge is South Waziristan," Karimov told a press conference. Suspects detained after a series of suicide bombings, explosions and assaults in the capital Tashkent and the central region of Bukhara had confessed that they had been in South Waziristan and that they had links to people operating there, said the President.

April 23, 2004: A suspected Pakistani terrorist, arrested in Australia, was reportedly plotting to black out the nation's largest city Sydney with a bomb attack on power supplies. Faheem Khalid Lodhi, arrested on April 22, planned to use a home-made bomb made of ammonium nitrate fertiliser to attack the electricity grid and was ordering the required chemicals under bogus company names. The Sydney Morning Herald reported that Lodhi hoped to disable the grid in Sydney, creating a blackout that would cause chaos in the city of four million people. Lodhi is the second member of a suspected terrorist cell arrested in a week after 21-year-old Pakistani-born medical student Izhar-ul-Haq. Both Lodhi and Haq were arrested as a result of investigations into terrorist suspect Willie Brigitte, a French national who was deported from Australia late last year, and is being detained by authorities in France who believe that he was setting up a terrorist cell in Sydney. Both Brigitte and Haq allegedly have links to the Pakistan-based

Lashkar-e-Toiba (LeT), which was designated as a terrorist organisation in Australia during November 2003.

April 18, 2004: US Ambassador to Afghanistan, Zalmay Khalilzad, said in Kabul that Al Qaeda, Taliban and Hizb-e-Islami elements were still in Pakistan and blamed them of cross-border terrorist activities. According to Khalilzad, "These elements attack the American forces, the Afghan forces and the NGOs working in Afghanistan...But it will not be good for Pakistan to become sanctuary for these people to plan, get training and come to Afghanistan with weapons." The envoy alleged that Al Qaeda and Taliban terrorists were in the Baluchistan area around Quetta while individuals were also in cities like Lahore, Karachi and Peshawar.

March 30, 2004: Police in London arrested eight Muslims believed to be of Pakistani origin along with a cache of explosives during raids on March 30. The eight men, all British citizens, were detained under the Terrorism Act 2000 for suspected involvement in planning a terrorist attack, said Peter Clarke, head of the Metropolitan Police anti-terrorist branch.

March 25, 2004: Daily Times reported that 163 terrorists had been arrested thus far in the ongoing military operations in Waziristan Agency. Interior Minister Hayat said that Arabs, Uzbeks and Chechens were among the foreign terrorists detained.

March 22, 2004: According to Dawn (Pakistani newspaper), the Polish police said that they had arrested two Pakistanis and a Ukrainian amid fears of a terrorist attack. "We have arrested two Pakistanis and one Ukrainian," police spokesperson Pawel Chojecki told AFP.

March 21, 2004: Zalmay Khalilzad, the US Ambassador to Afghanistan, said in Kabul that the Taliban are still plotting attacks on Afghan and US targets from safe havens in Pakistan. "We know several key Taliban figures are there and there is some sense that some of the remaining Al Qaeda leaders are in the border area on the other side," said Khalizad.

March 20, 2004: Security forces have reportedly arrested at least 100 "foreign" terrorists and the local Pashtuns sheltering them in the Waziristan agency on the Pakistan-Afghanistan border in the ongoing offensive in search of Al Qaeda and Taliban suspects. Unconfirmed reports indicated that dozens of Al Qaeda suspects and their supporters were killed during the operations. "Over 100 people have been arrested including a certain number of foreigners," Peshawar Corps Commander Lt Gen Safdar Hussain told reporters in Wana.

March 15, 2004: President Pervez Musharraf said in Peshawar that the master-minds behind terrorist attacks in the country and the suicide attempts on his life were hiding in the tribal belt along the Afghanistan border. "We have busted a complete network and found leads that a Libyan national was involved in the sui-cide attempts on my life. He has not been arrested so far and we also still don't know who ordered the attacks," said the President. He also said that Pakistanis were being recruited, trained in terrorism and offered millions of rupees by these elements to carry out suicide missions. According to Musharraf, "We have infor-mation that 500 to 600 foreign nationals were staying in our country, especially in South Waziristan."

March 4, 2004: Three American Muslims belonging to what the US Govern-ment calls a "Virginia jihad" were convicted of conspiracy to wage war on Amer-ica and provide material support to the Taliban, charges that carry possible life imprisonment. US Attorney General John Ashcroft said in Washington that the convictions were handed down against Masoud Khan, Abdur Raheem and Seifulla Chapman in US District Court in Alexandria, Virginia, by Judge Leonie Brinkema. "The defendants convicted today were associates of Lashkar-e-Taiba," said Ashcroft.

March 1, 2004: Security agencies in Peshawar are reported to have arrested eight Al Qaeda suspects over the past two days. While two suspects were arrested from Zangali Police Checkpost in the Badabeer area after a brief encounter, at least six more, including three Algerians and three Afghans, were arrested at the Kacha Ghari refugee camp.

February 28, 2004: According to Nation (Pakistani newspaper), the United States has handed over to Pakistan a list of 53 Al Qaeda suspects believed to be hiding in South Waziristan bordering Afghanistan. "The Bush administration has extended a list to Pakistani authorities which contain the names of 53 al-Qaeda suspects who, it said, have taken refuge in South Waziristan Agency. This US contention is based on intelligence reports gathered from Afghanistan that these suspected terrorists have sneaked into the Pakistani side a couple of months ago," the report indicated.

February 25, 2004: Information Minister Sheikh Rashid Ahmed said in Lahore that Al Qaeda chief Osama bin Laden and his deputy Ayman-al-Zawahri were in Afghanistan or in the area of Pakistan-Afghanistan border.

February 24, 2004: Pakistani security agencies launched an operation against suspected terrorists taking shelter in the tribal areas bordering Afghanistan. At least 20 Al Qaeda suspects, including some foreign nationals, are reported to have been arrested during these raids. Director General of Inter Services Public Relations (ISPR) Maj. Gen Shaukat Sultan said that foreign nationals were among those captured in the Azam Warsak and Shkai areas. Benazir Bhutto claimed in London on February 24 that she was approached several times when she was Pakistani Prime Minister by military officials and scientists seeking permission to export nuclear technology, but she had turned down their requests. In an interview to the Financial Times, Bhutto said she and senior military officers had agreed to bar the export of nuclear technology in December 1988.

February 18, 2004: Zalmay Khalizad, US Special Envoy to Afghanistan, has reportedly charged that the Taliban, Al Qaeda and Gulbuddin Hikmatyar's supporters keep "coming across from Pakistan" into Afghanistan. He was speaking by a satellite phone from Kabul to a conference on Afghanistan organised by the US Institute for Peace.

February 13, 2004: Three Al Qaeda suspects were arrested consequent to a shootout in the Jamrud tribal area near the Afghan border, in which three persons were injured. The arrests come after security agencies captured an equal number of suspects, including two Arabs, on February 12. During the shootout, an Arab suspect was injured when he attempted to blow himself up with a grenade, said local official Riaz Khan. He added that the arrests were made at the house of a tribesman, identified as Mohammad Amin, who was also among those arrested.

February 10, 2004: The Washington Times reported that the Al Qaeda is training hundreds of Islamist radicals in Pakistan and Kashmir to send them to "sleeper cells" in the US. Quoting unnamed American and foreign officials, the report said that at least 400 radicals have been trained or are in training in special camps, and many have already been routed through Europe to Muslim communities in US. US intelligence officials were quoted as saying that the camps operate in remote regions of western Pakistan and in Pakistan occupied Kashmir (PoK) and are financed by various terrorist networks, including the Al Qaeda and sources in Saudi Arabia. Training camps in PoK were reportedly being operated by the Harkat-ul-Ansar and Lashkar-e-Toiba.

January 27, 2004: According to Dawn (Pakistani newspaper), a close aide to the Taliban leader, Mulla Mohammad Omar, was arrested in Chaman, a town near the Afghan border. Interior Minister Faisal Saleh Hayat said that the man arrested near the border town of Chaman, some 470km southwest of Islamabad, was Abdul Mannan Khawajazai, a former provincial governor during Taliban rule in Afghanistan from 1996 to 2001.

January 22, 2004: Intelligence agencies arrested Al Qaeda operative, Ibad Al Yaquti Al Sheikh Al Sufiyan, at Rabia City apartments in Gulistan-e-Jauhar, Karachi. Two satellite phones, one mobile phone, one laptop computer and two passports were recovered from Al Yaquti's possession. Al Yaquti is a resident of Dammam in Saudi Arabia.

January 21, 2004: According to the Daily Times, members of the intelligence agencies raided a flat in a residential project in Karachi's Gulistan-e-Jauhar and arrested Walid bin Azmi, an Al Qaeda operative. Azmi is believed to be one of the four suspects involved in the bombing of US navy ship USS Cole on October 12, 2000.

January 18, 2004: Police arrested seven people in Karachi's Gulistan-e-Jauhar area on suspicion that they were linked to Al Qaeda or another terrorist organisation, the Daily Times reported. The arrested persons include two Egyptians, three Afghans and two women along with three children. The report added that the police recovered 11 hand grenades, four handguns, ammunition and maps of Afghanistan and Pakistan from the possession of the arrested persons.

December 17, 2003: A Pakistani national, who received training to join the Lashkar-e-Toiba (LeT) in the Indian State of Jammu and Kashmir, has reportedly been sentenced in the United States to 10 years and six months in prison. Mohammad Aatique, was the first to be sentenced among a group of 11 people indicted in Pennsylvania and Virginia in July 2003 for training with assault rifles. Aatique had entered into a plea bargain with the prosecution under which he pleaded guilty of going to Pakistan after the September 11, 2001, terrorist attacks to train with the LeT. A US Federal Court in Pennsylvania on December 17 sentenced Aatique to the mandatory 10 years for firearms violations and six months for conspiring to violate the US Neutrality Act. Among the remaining suspects, three have pleaded guilty to weapons charges and the trial is expected to commence in February 2004.

December 10, 2003: After the recent suicide attacks in Turkey, the United States has asked the Government of Pakistan to add names of 15 more people to the consolidated list of people and entities belonging to Taliban and al-Qaeda, Dawn (Pakistani newspaper) has learnt. The source said the government had been provided with the list endorsed by the United Nations and asked to freeze the assets of the people included in it, seal their offices and prevent their entry or transit. The 15 people to be added in the list are Al-Ayashi Radiabdul Al-Sami (Egypt), Cabullah (Somalia), Hamid M Tahir (Iraq), Mustafa Muhammad Amin (Iraq), M Daki (Morocco), Al-Sadi Furgh Hassan (Libya), Sadi Nasir (Tunisia), Ben Abdul Hakim (Tunisia), Reham Lutfi (Tunisia), Bouyahia Hamadi (Morocco), Rown lazher Bin Khalifa Bin Ahmed (Tunisia), Zarkavi Imed Bin Maki (Tunisia), Murad Trablsi (Tunisia), Kamal Bin Mauldi (Tunisia) and Nauriddi Drissi (Tunisia).

November 29, 2003: Afghan President Hamid Karzai claimed that Taliban chief Mullah Mohammed Omar was seen at Quetta in Pakistan last week. Karzai told London-based The Times that he had received information that Mullah Omar was spotted praying in a mosque in Quetta. Karzai also said that Quetta was a stronghold for Islamist extremists opposing the coalition forces in Afghanistan.

November 20, 2003: According to The Turkish Daily News, Turkish police have indicated that three of the four suicide bombers who carried out the November 15, 2003, blasts at two synagogues had received training in Pakistan during the nineteen nineties. The report said that the police found pieces of a Pakistani passport suspected to belong to one of the attackers. At least 23 persons were killed in the attacks.

November 14,2003: Abdul Qadir, a close associate of the Taliban chief Mullah Omar, is arrested from his residence at the University Town area in Peshawar.

November 7, 2003: Australian Parliament passes a bill to outlaw the Pakistan-based Lashkar-e-Toiba. The move to designate LeT as a terrorist outfit came after allegations that a French terror suspect deported to Paris in October 2003 had trained with the group.

November 3, 2003: Two suspected Uzbek terrorists are killed during an encounter with Pakistani troops in the Angoor Adda area of South Waziristan Agency. October 25:

Security agencies arrest two Yemenis and a Pakistani from Faisalabad for suspected links to the Al Qaeda network.

October 16, 2003: The United States designates Pakistan-based Indian Mafia don Dawood Ibrahim as a global terrorist having links with the Al Qaeda and financing activities of the Lashkar-e-Toiba and other terrorist groups.

October 14, 2003: Karachi-based Al Akhtar Trust is designated as a Global Terrorist entity by the US Treasury.

October 8, 2003: US Federal prosecutors formally charge a Pakistani national with providing material support to the Al Qaeda, more than six months after his arrest in New York City.

October 2, 2003: At least 12 Al Qaeda terrorists are killed and 18 others arrested during an operation launched by the Pakistan Army in the remote South Waziristan Agency (SWA), close to the Afghanistan border. Two Pakistani soldiers were also reportedly killed and two others injured during the encounter.

September 22, 2003: Media reports indicate that Gun Gun Rusman Gunawan, younger brother of Hambali, chief of the Indonesian terrorist group Jemaah Islamiyyah, was arrested from the Gulshan-e-Iqbal area in Karachi a month back.

September 20, 2003: Security agencies reportedly raided two Madrassas (seminaries) in Karachi and arrested 16 foreigners for suspected links to various extremist groups. The raids occurred at the Jamia Abi Bakar and Madrasa Dar-ul-Islam seminaries in the Gulshan-e-Iqbal area of Karachi. Among those arrested were 13 Malaysian, two Indonesian and a Burmese.

September 15, 2003: Declassified US intelligence documents reportedly reveal that Pakistan helped Al Qaeda terrorists launch their operations in Afghanistan in the 1990s and also clandestinely ran a major training camp used by Osama Bin Laden's network.

September 12, 2003: Islamist separatists in China's Muslim northwest are securing assistance from international terrorists, including instruction in "several training camps in Pakistan," claims Wang Lequan, the region's Communist Party secretary.

August 8, 2003: US authorities charge Uzair Paracha, a Pakistani national, with conspiring to provide financial and other assistance to the Al Qaeda.

July 15, 2003: Suspected Al Qaeda terrorist, Adil Al-Jazeeri, arrested in June 2003, is handed over to American authorities in Peshawar.

July 4, 2003: Security agencies raid a village in the coastal area of Ghorabari in the Thatta district and arrest six persons, including the head of a Madrassa (seminary) and a woman, on suspicion of their links with the Al Qaeda. A wireless set, sensitive maps of the coastal area and sea routes, a rifle and two life jackets were recovered from the incident site.

June 27, 2003: Eight persons, accused of planning terrorist acts in the Indian State of Jammu and Kashmir, are arrested during a series of raids around the US Federal Capital of Washington, the US Justice Department said in a statement. Three other persons, reportedly living in Saudi Arabia, were also named in a 42-count Justice Department indictment. Initial appearances are to commence in the US Federal Court in Alexandria, Virginia, before Judge Rawles Jones, said US Attorney Paul McNulty. The accused have been indicted on conspiracy, firearms and other charges for alleged roles in a conspiracy to train and participate in Jehad in Kashmir in support of the proscribed Lashkar-e-Toiba (LeT). They have also been accused of conspiring to prepare for and engage in Jehad in Chechnya, the Philippines and other countries. The group reportedly obtained AK-47 rifles and practiced small-unit military tactics in Virginia using paintball weapons and items to simulate actual combat in preparation for Jehad, said the Justice Department. The indictment said that some of the defendants traveled to Pakistan and trained with the LeT, listed by the US among terrorist organisations. The suspects were arrested in the States of Maryland, Virginia and Pennsylvania, an unnamed Federal Bureau of Investigation (FBI) official said adding they were named as Randall Todd Royer; Yemeni national Ibrahim Ahmad al-Hamdi; Masood Ahmad Khan; naturalized US citizen Yong Ki Kwon; Pakistani national Muhammad Aatiq; Hammad Abdur-Raheem; Donald Thomas Surratt; and Caliph Basha Ibn Abdur Raheem. Three others—Khwaja Mahmood Hasan, a Pakistani-born US citizen; Sabri Benkhala; and Seifullah Chapman—are believed to be in Saudi Arabia.

June 17, 2003: Security agencies arrest an Arab national along with three Afghans suspected of having links with the Al Qaeda from Peshawar (Pakistan). Official sources were quoted as saying in reports that Adil al-Jazeeri, an Algerian national, was arrested from Peshawar's Hayatabad locality along with three others. "He is a big catch. He is known among the Arabs for his close links with al-Qaeda," said an unnamed official. Adil al-Jazeeri is reportedly on the US list of wanted Arab nationals believed to be close associates of bin Laden.

June 5, 2003: Michael Evanoff, Regional Security Officer of the US Embassy in Islamabad (Pakistan) told the Christian Science Monitor that, "This [Pakistan] is now the epicentre of terrorism. It really is. This is the only country I know in the world that has so many groups that are against the US or Western ideals. Last year alone, these groups pulled off seven strikes against the US community here, including a March church bombing in Islamabad that killed five—among them an American woman from the embassy and her daughter—and a June truck bomb at the Karachi consulate that killed 14 Pakistanis."

June 1, 2003: Daily Times reports that Pakistan's security agencies are hunting for an Afghan national Hamdullah, popularly known as Mufti Inaam, who was the head of the intelligence agency under the erstwhile Taliban regime and has close contacts with bin Laden. Mufti Inaam reportedly distanced himself from the government shortly after the 9/11 attacks and consequent to the US military campaign in Afghanistan, he crossed the border and hid in the northwestern region of Pakistan. He is suspected to have remained underground in Peshawar for quite some time and also helped many of his friends and colleagues in Afghanistan enter Pakistan through safe routes before the fall of Kandahar. He is also believed to have assisted many Arab families migrate to Pakistan and arranged their safe settlements in various parts of the country. In Pakistan, Mufti Inaam remained in contact with certain terrorist groups and Al Qaeda operatives for many months.

May 27, 2003: Security agencies arrest a suspected Afghan Al Qaeda operative during a raid in the northwestern tribal territory bordering Afghanistan. The suspect, identified as Abdullah, was apprehended in a pre-dawn raid in Shahkas village near the border town of Jamrud, 25 km west of Peshawar, an unnamed official was quoted as saying in a media report.

May 15, 2003: Three suspected Al Qaeda operatives, including an Arab, are arrested in Karachi. The foreign national, identified as Iffan-ul-Hassham, was detained during an overnight raid at a hideout on the outskirts of Karachi during which a laptop computer and a satellite phone were seized. Two more men, both Pakistanis, were later detained based on information provided by Hassham.

May 11, 2003: Police in Peshawar (Pakistan) unearth a passport-selling racket that was supplying stolen Pakistani passports to Al Qaeda suspects. An unspecified number of arrests were made on May 11 in Peshawar, said Inamullah Khan Gandapur, an Assistant Director with the Federal Investigations Agency, which polices immigration. "We had seen information that these people were involved in providing Pakistani passports to al-Qaeda suspects," Gandapur said. Police seized 100 blank Pakistani passports, which were earlier stolen from a government office in Swat.

May 8, 2003: Taliban sources in Pakistan and Afghan intelligence sources indicate that the Taliban currently has a recognizable hierarchy of leaders—some operating from Afghanistan and some from the Pashtun tribal areas of Pakistan's Northwest Frontier Province (NWFP). In Pakistan, Taliban commanders are reportedly working in alliance with like-minded leaders of Islamist extremist parties who now control two provinces along the Afghan-Pakistan border. In the NWFP, Qari Akhtar is the chief operations commander; in the Tor Ghar mountains near the Afghan border town of Spin Boldak, Mullah Mohammad Ibrahim is the Taliban's top leader. Shahzada Zulfikar, a Quetta-based political analyst, says that Taliban commanders continue to receive support from Pakistan's intelligence agencies, as they did more openly during the Taliban government. "The Taliban were and are still friends of Pakistan," says Zulfikar. "Pakistan ditched the Taliban due to American pressure, for a while, but now there are fears that their relationship might be restored due to the increasing presence of Indians in Afghanistan." Taliban activists in Pakistan and Afghanistan claim that they are receiving direct assistance from Pakistan's Islamist parties, including Jamaat-e-Islami and the Jamiat-Ulema-e-Islam. "We are at home as we were before (President) Musharraf hatched a conspiracy against us at the behest of the Americans," says Mir Jan, a Taliban fighter in Quetta. "But our brothers [the mullahs] are in power, so it means we are in power."

May 9, 2003: Security agencies in Karachi arrest two suspected members of the Taliban militia, including a close associate of the ousted regime's former Ambassador to Pakistan, during a raid. The authorities also seized a satellite phone, a sub-machinegun and an unspecified amount of foreign currency from their possession.

May 3, 2003: Police in Karachi arrest two Egyptian Al Qaeda suspects from Surjani Town and seized three AK-47 assault rifles, two TT pistols, two satellite phones, some transmitters and refined explosives from their possession. The two suspects, Abdul Khaliq Muhammad and Abi Abdullah, were reportedly planning to attack the US marines at Shahbaz airbase in Jacobabad, Miran Shah Airport and other sensitive installations in Gwadar.

May 2, 2003: Pakistani authorities handed over three Arab Al Qaeda suspects, including prime suspect in the October 2000-USS Cole bombing, Waleed Muhammad Bin Attash alias Khalid Al-Attash, to the US officials. Although the government did not officially confirm the extradition, an unnamed official was quoted as saying that "the foreigners including Al-Attash are not in our custody. They were handed over to the Americans." Bin Attash is a nephew of front ranking Al Qaeda terrorist Khalid Sheikh Muhammad, who was arrested on March 1, 2003, from Rawalpindi. Official sources claimed that Al-Attash and other suspects were not wanted by Pakistan in any criminal case and they were handed over to the US owing to the fact that the suspects were reportedly involved in terrorist acts aimed at the US establishments. May 1:

President Pervez Musharraf said in Islamabad that there were indications that Osama bin Laden was alive, and may be hiding in the tribal territory on the Pakistani-Afghan border. In an interview to a private television channel he said, "some indications are there that he is not dead but where is he? Nothing can be said about that…If they are in a small group, two, four, eight or 10 people, then they can hide in this side, our side of the tribal area, or hide on the Afghan side. I cannot say with surety."

April 30, 2003: Eleven Al Qaeda suspects, including three Arabs, were arrested from different parts of Karachi. Police also seized a large cache of arms, ammunition and explosives from their possession. An unnamed official was quoted as saying that the arrested men were reportedly planning to attack the US Consulate, American establishments and government installations. An Interior Ministry statement issued from Islamabad said "six suspects have been arrested which include Waleed Muhammad Bin Attash alias Khalid Al-Attash, a Yemeni national, who is suspected to be involved in the US Ship Cole incident." According to the statement, some 200 detonators, one wrist watch timer switch, five touch switches, capacitors of various types, 20 diodes, 46 transmitters, 20 variable controls, Kalashnikovs, hand grenades, pistols, ammunition and a truck load of sulphur, gunpowder and urea bags were recovered.

April 23, 2003: Afghanistan has begun submitting lists of wanted "war criminals and terrorists" to Pakistan in an effort to stamp out Taliban and Al Qaeda cadres lurking along the neighbours' mountainous border, said Afghan President Hamid Karzai in Islamabad. "We are going to come up with a more specific list of names who will be considered criminals of war against the Afghan people. There are people who are definitely terrorists." He named Akhtar Mohammad Usmani, a deputy of Taliban leader Mullah Omar, Mullah Dadullah, the Taliban's intelligence chief, Mullah Biradar, the militia's internal security chief and Hafiz Mujeeb, a lower-ranking commander. Many Afghan officials, suspicious of Pakistan for its previous nurturing and support of the Taliban regime, have accused it of allowing sanctuary for fugitive extremists in its remote tribal border regions.

April 18, 2003: Ugandan military intelligence chief Colonel Nobel Mayombo was quoted as saying in the Daily Times that "All along even before the US-led war in Iraq, we had intelligence reports that Ugandan terrorist groups were sending their recruits to centres in Iraq, Sudan, Pakistan and Afghanistan."

April 16, 2003: According to a media report, pamphlets urging Afghan refugees to wage Jehad against US forces and their "hireling" government in Afghanistan have been circulated at camps in northwest Pakistan. Entitled "Declaration by the Islamic Emirate of Afghanistan" (IEA) the leaflets, written in Pushto, were distributed this week at refugee camps in the North West Frontier Province (NWFP) bordering Afghanistan. The erstwhile Taliban regime had ruled Afghanistan under the rubric of IEA, headed by Mullah Mohammad Omar. "Ulema, tribal leaders and Mujahideen of IEA call upon you to wage jihad against the hireling government in your motherland. It is your duty to rise…and direct your swords against the infidels and their puppets," said the leaflets.

April 8, 2003: Pakistani security agencies arrested a medical practitioner and his son for suspected links to the Al Qaeda network. M Khan Mahmood Ahmed Kathia and his son were reportedly arrested from Banni Qasim area, in Harrapa.

April 7, 2003: According to a media report, two Pakistani Al Qaeda suspects were arrested from a village near Sahiwal in Multan. The Interior Ministry, however, claimed it was unaware of the arrests.

April 3, 2003: Pakistani security agencies, in association with US Federal Bureau of Investigation (FBI) agents, arrested two suspected Al Qaeda operatives in

Peshawar. Information Minister Sheikh Rashid said the arrested "have been identified as Abdullah and Abdul Karim." Officials in Peshawar were quoted as saying
that both came from Middle Eastern countries. They are also allegedly linked to
the killing of Sher Nawaz Khan, an officer of the Inter Services Intelligence (ISI),
Pakistan's external intelligence agency, in March 2003 at Wana, 180 miles south
of Peshawar.

March 28, 2003: A Pakistani woman, who was on the US Federal Bureau of
Investigation (FBI) list for suspected links to the Al Qaeda, was arrested from the
Gulshan-e-Iqbal area in Karachi. According to a media report, Dr Aafia Siddiqui
was allegedly working with the 'Chemical Wire Group' of the Al Qaeda.
Recently, the FBI had placed the photograph of Aafia Siddiqui at its website stating "Although the FBI has no information indicating this individual is connected
to specific terrorist activities, the FBI would like to locate and question this individual." As reported earlier, Aafia having a doctorate degree in neurological sci-
ences from the Massachusetts Institute of Technology, was living in Boston along
with her spouse and three children. She is alleged to have provided logistical support to a Saudi Al Qaeda operative Adnan G El Shukrijumah.

March 27, 2003: The Supreme Court of Pakistan held that the country lacks a
law declaring Al Qaeda a terrorist organization and, consequently, no one could
be detained simply for having links with the organization. The Supreme Court
made the observation in a judgment on the Federal Government's appeal against
an earlier Lahore High Court order of releasing three Al Qaeda suspects. "Our
security laws and anti-terrorism enactments are silent to the affect that Al Qaeda
is a terrorist organization, having its network at global level and that it is a furious
threat to national/international peace, security and tranquility," said the apex
court.

March 18, 2003: Two suspected Al Qaeda operatives of Arab origin are arrested
from the campus of Peshawar's main university.

March 17, 2003: Six suspected Al Qaeda operatives are arrested in Lahore.
Among those arrested were Yasir al Jaziri's brother-in-law, a Qatari national and
at least three Afghans.

March 15, 2003: Pakistani authorities arrested a leading Al Qaeda terrorist,
Moroccan national Yasir al-Jaziri, in Lahore. The arrest was based on information
given by Khalid Sheikh Mohammed, the suspected mastermind of 9/11 attacks,

who was arrested from Rawalpindi on March 1. "He (al-Jaziri) is less important than Khalid Sheikh Mohammed but he is quite an important person," Secretary of the Interior Ministry Tasneem Noorani was quoted as saying. Al-Jaziri is suspected to be involved in Al Qaeda's business operations and an unnamed official is quoted as describing him as an US-educated "computer whiz". He had also played a significant role in disseminating audio and videotapes of Osama bin Laden to the media.

March 9, 2003: An Iraqi and two Afghan nationals were arrested in Hyderabad, Sindh province, for suspected Al Qaeda links. They are also suspected to be involved in the murder of an official of the Inter-Services Intelligence (ISI), Pakistan's external intelligence agency, in Wana, South Waziristan, on March 4.

March 1, 2003: Three Al Qaeda terrorists, including the suspected mastermind behind 9/11, Khalid Sheikh Mohammed, were arrested in Rawalpindi on March 1. Kuwaiti-born Khalid, who is on the most wanted list of the Federal Bureau of Investigation (FBI) of the US, is regarded as a key Al Qaeda lieutenant and organizer of the September 11 attacks in the US. The US government had announced a $25 million reward for information leading to his capture. He is a relative of Ramzi Ahmed Yousef, now serving a life sentence for involvement in the 1993 World Trade Centre bombing. On March 2, Khalid was handed over to the US authorities.

February 17, 2003: Ali Imran, a key suspect in the Bali bombings, reportedly confessed that he spent 18 months at a Madrassa in Peshawar before entering Afghanistan to conduct "jihad."
(Comment: This Ali Imran also spent time with Tablighi Jamat in Raiwind and was brainwashed to enter Afghan jihad)

February 13, 2003: An Egyptian national was arrested from the Wahadat colony in Quetta (Pakistan) on charges of having links with the Al Qaeda network.

January 17, 2003: Two Tajik and two Arab operatives of the Al Qaeda are arrested in Karachi.

January 12, 2003: A 'military commander' of Afghanistan's former Prime Minister and warlord Gulbuddin Hekmatyar, was arrested from his residence in the Baghgai village, approximately 15km away from Wana in Peshawar, for suspected links with the Al Qaeda.

January 8, 2003: Abu Omar, hailing from Morocco, and Abu Hamza, belonging to Yemen, were arrested after an encounter in the Gulshan-i-Maymar area of Karachi. Omar was trying to establish a Pakistan Sector of the Al Qaeda and was in constant contact with Khalid Sheikh Mohammed, suspected mastermind behind the 9/11 attacks. January 4: Jack Thomas, a 29-year-old Australian convert to Islam, was arrested in Karachi for suspected links to the Al Qaeda. He was reportedly in contact with Al Qaeda operatives who had managed to sneak into Karachi. Information gleaned from Thomas led to the arrest of two men of Arab origin from a house in Karachi on January 9, five days after Thomas was arrested. The two men, identified as an Iraqi and Jordanian-Palestinian, were captured from a hose on Karachi's outskirts. A third Al Qaeda suspect escaped, leaving behind an Algerian passport.

December 21, 2002: According to Major Stephen Clutter, a US military spokesperson at the Bagram Air Base in Afghanistan, suspected Al Qaeda terrorists who killed a US soldier on December 21 near the village of Shkin, about 60 km south of Gardez, Afghanistan, had fled across the eastern border into Pakistan.

December 18, 2002: Ahmed Javed Khawaja, a medical practitioner, is arrested along with four of his relatives for harbouring Al Qaeda terrorists at his residence in Lahore. According to an Interior Ministry statement in the Lahore court (submitted in January 2003) the terrorists harboured by the family were Abu Yasir Al Jaziri, identified as an Algerian or Moroccan, Assadullah and Sheikh Said Al-Misri, both listed as Egyptians and Abu Faraj, listed as North African. Al Jaziri was "responsible for the business of al-Qaeda," Al-Misri was a financial chief of the network, and Faraj was the head of Al Qaeda's North Africa network, according to the statement. Faraj was also a deputy of Khalid Sheikh Mohammed, suspected mastermind of the 9/11 attacks. Ahmed Khawaja also reportedly confessed that he provided medical treatment to a wife of Osama bin Laden and also to the wife of another key Al Qaeda leader, Abu Zubaida. The FBI discovered Khawaja's links with the Al Qaeda by tracing the Internet channels allegedly being used by him. He has been charged with providing treatment and financial support to Al Qaeda operatives and is alleged to have visited Kabul after 9/11. According to media reports, Khawaja had often visited Afghanistan during the war against the former Soviet Union and had collected funds for war victims at that time.

December 4, 2002: Pakistani security agencies arrested two Al Qaeda suspects in South Waziristan Agency, and have reportedly handed them over to American intelligence agencies for interrogation. They have been arrested for alleged involvement in an attack on a US military camp in southern Paktika province of Afghanistan.

November 29, 2002: Canadian government, acting on sustained pressure from the parliamentary Opposition, designated the Pakistan-based Jaish-e-Moham-med (JeM) and Harkat-ul-Mujahideen (HuM) as terrorist groups.

November 26, 2002: French Police claim arrest of several Pakistani nationals during a raid in Paris. They are suspected associates of shoe-bomber Richard Reid. They were reportedly arrested at a Pakistani cultural center as well as at a restaurant and a mosque. Meanwhile, during a parallel raid at the Reunion Island, a French department located in the Indian Ocean, a former Imam (priest) of the Ali Mosque, also a Pakistani national, was also arrested and is scheduled to undergo questioning by French police.

November 18, 2002: Benevolence International Foundation (BIF), an interna-tional Non-governmental Organisation (NGO), with offices in Islamabad and Peshawar was officially declared as a terrorist group by the US authorities. The Office of Foreign Assets Control (OFAC) USA said, on November 18, BIF has been officially listed as a "Specially Designated Global Terrorist."

November 10, 2002: The French police indicated that order was given in Karachi for the April 11, 2002-suicide attack on a synagogue in Djerba, in Tunisia. The attack resulted in the death of 21 persons, including two French and 14 German tourists. French anti-terrorist police who have been investigating the attack said they have ascertained that the satellite telephone used by the suicide terrorist, Nizar Naouar, who drove an explosives-laden truck into the synagogue, was acquired in Paris by Walid Naouar, Nizar's brother, who is being interrogated by police in Lyons. Police have claimed that the last telephonic call by Nizar before undertaking the attack was to a number in Karachi that has been identified as that of Khaled Sheikh Mohammad, a Kuwaiti and one of the new 'operational heads' of the Al Qaeda.

November 8, 2002: The US State Department added nine more groups sus-pected of terrorist links to a visa blacklist that will keep their members or affiliates out of the country. Among the newly named entities is the Pakistan-based Ummah Tamir-e-Nau (UTN), an organisation whose chief Dr. Sultan Bashirud-din Mahmood, former Director General of the Pakistan Atomic Energy Commission, was arrested on October 23, 2001, in Islamabad along with his associate Abdul Majeed (arrested in Lahore) for their alleged links to the Al Qaeda.

November 6, 2002: Three Pakistani men have been arrested in California for attempting to supply US-made Stinger missiles to the Al Qaeda terrorist network, US Attorney General John Ashcroft said on November 6. Ashcroft said the three were trafficking 600 kilos of heroin and five tonnes of hashish to purchase the shoulder-fired anti-aircraft missiles. "Three individuals have been indicted for conspiring to trade heroin for anti-aircraft missiles which they said they intended to sell to Al-Qaeda forces in Afghanistan," said Ashcroft.

October 30, 2002: A report indicated that of the six new Al Qaeda leaders, who the United States believes are currently in active command of the group, one is said to be residing in Pakistan and two in the Pakistan-Afghanistan border region. The three terrorists are Saif al-Adel alias Makkawi, an Egyptian, Abdullah Ahmed Abdullah alias Abu Mohammed al Masri, Al Qaeda's 'financial officer' and Tawfiq bin Atash alias Khallad, Al Qaeda's 'senior operational planner'. While the first two are believed to be in the Pakistan-Afghanistan border region, the last is reportedly in Pakistan.

October 18, 2002: Islamabad police and FBI agents arrested Iranian lecturer Habibullah Zaiee of International Islamic University for his alleged links with the Al Qaeda. A media report indicated that Zaiee was suspected of involvement in co-ordinating the attacks on US installations in the country in the recent past.

October 15, 2002: Four Afghan refugees were arrested in a joint raid conducted by local police and US Federal Bureau of Investigation (FBI) agents at the Jalozai Refugee Camp, Peshawar, on the suspicion that they had links with the Al Qaeda. The Jalozai Refugee Camp is run by the Ittehad-e-Islami Afghanistan, a group consisting of erstwhile Afghan fighters who fought against the erstwhile Soviet Union in the 1980s.

October 8, 2002: Two Afghans are arrested from the Shamshato refugee camp on the charge of providing shelter to some Al Qaeda suspects.

September 22, 2002: Police arrested five Al Qaeda suspects in Peshawar and Mianwali. Of them, an Al Qaeda member and two others were arrested by a joint-team of Crime Investigation Department (CID) and Inter-Services Intelligence (ISI) sleuths from Peshawar's Jehangirabad area, while two others were arrested from Mianwali. Official sources in Peshawar said, of the three-arrested, one is a Tunisian, one belongs to the Nooristan province of Afghanistan while the third is a Pakistani.

September 12, 2002: Italian police working with US naval intelligence said they had arrested 15 Pakistanis, suspected to be members of the Al Qaeda terrorist network. They were reportedly taken into custody in August 2002 after arriving in the southern Sicilian port town of Gela on a merchant cargo ship from Morocco. They have been charged with conspiracy to commit terrorist acts. "We are certain that these people are part of a terrorist organization, and we are almost certain that that organization is Al Qaeda," said Santi Giuffre, chief of police for the Sicilian province of Caltanissetta. He also said police had seized telephone numbers, including several in Spain and France, which linked these men to the Al Qaeda. Notes and documents referring to the Al Qaeda were reportedly found on-board their Romanian-registered vessel, which set sail from Casablanca in mid-July and was scheduled to visit Tunisia, Malta and the Libyan capital of Tripoli. All men were carrying an open, return air ticket from Karachi to Casablanca, he added.

September 11, 2002: Ramzi Binalshibh, Al Qaeda terrorist and a 9/11 prime suspect was detained in Karachi. Two suspected Al Qaeda terrorists were killed and five others, including Binalshibh, were arrested after a three-hour encounter at Defence Housing Authority in Karachi. The encounter ensued when security forces raided an apartment C-63 of a complex on 15th Street, Phase II Extension. Binalshibh, a Yemeni, was arrested with assistance from the FBI. Binalshibh, wanted in Germany for his alleged role in planning and carrying out the 9/11 attacks, is one of the front-ranking Al Qaeda terrorists to be taken into custody over the past year. In an interview to the Al Jazeera, he had reportedly claimed that he was an active planner of the 9/11 attacks. US officials have indicated that Binalshibh, also known as Ramzi bin al-Shaibah, was refused visa to enter the US at least four times before 9/11. He reportedly wanted to join the 19 hijackers involved in the multiple terrorist attacks. He was also reportedly one of the roommates of Mohamed Atta—the suspected leader of the 9/11 hijackers—in Hamburg, Germany. He had played a key role in the transmission of funds to the terrorists undergoing flying training in the USA.

August 30, 2002: According to a report in Dawn, a Pakistani daily, one of the most-wanted men in Uzbekistan is in hiding near the Pakistan border but cannot be extradited despite a treaty between the two countries. Quoting Uzbekistan President Islam Karimov, Uzbek Embassy officials in Washington said that Tohir

Yoldashev, political and ideological leader of the Islamic Movement of Uzbekistan (IMU), was hiding near the Afghanistan-Pakistan border, but from time to time he lived in Pakistan as well. In year 2000, the Uzbek Supreme Court had, in absentia, sentenced Yoldashev to death. Terrorist group IMU is a coalition of Islamist terrorists from Uzbekistan and other Central Asian countries who are opposed to Karimov's regime.

August 18, 2002: Police in Peshawar arrested five Somalis near the Afghanistan border for suspected links with the Al Qaeda.

August 17, 2002: The then Interior Minister Moinuddin Haider said that "58 prisoners of Pakistani origin are at present registered to be at the Guantanamo Base in Cuba." They were arrested in the wake of a crack-down by United States in the post-9/11 operations targeting persons linked with the Al Qaeda.

August 2, 2002: US authorities placed six Pakistanis on the list of suspected terrorists, businesses and organisations that are suspected of supporting terrorism. The US Treasury's Office of Foreign Assets Control (OFAC) has issued a new list of specially designated nationals and other persons, whose property is blocked worldwide, in order to assist the public in complying with various sanctions and programmes undertaken by the US government. One of them, Zia Ahmad, was linked to the multiple terrorist attacks on September 11, 2001 in the USA. The six Pakistanis mentioned in the list are: Zia Ahmad, a resident of Peshawar; Saiyid Abd Al-Man'am alias Agha Haji Abdul Manan; Nasir Ali Khan; Abdul Majid Chaudhry; Haji Ibrahim Khan Afridi and Mohammad Aziz. Furthermore, assets of the Pakistan-Libya Holding Company, Karachi, have been blocked as per the new list, while two new organisations have been listed as suspects in Pakistan, namely Revival of Islamic Society Heritage on the African continent, Pakistan office and Maktaba Al-Khidmat Al-Kifah, Peshawar. Other organisations and Pakistani nationals on the OFAC list include Lashkar-e-Toiba, Afghan Support Committee, Ahyaul Turas, Jamiat Ayat-ur-Rhas Al Islamia, Jamiat Ihya ul Turath Al Islamia, Jaish-e-Mohammed, Ladehyanoy, Mufti Mohammed Rashid, Ummah Tamir-e-Nau, Rabita Trust and Sultan Bashiruddin Mahmood.

July 27, 2002: A FBI team along with Pakistan Rangers raided a house in Luqman Mohallah in Khairpur and arrested four foreigners, suspected to be linked with the Al Qaeda. July 18:

Security agencies in Peshawar arrested 12 foreigners, suspecting them of having connections with the Al Qaeda. Out of those arrested five were Somalians, two Sudanese and one Afghan national, while the nationality of four could not be ascertained. They were arrested from the localities of University Town and Hayatabad Township in Peshawar.

July 15, 2002: An Anti-Terrorism Court in Hyderabad awarded death sentence to Ahmed Omar Saeed Sheikh and life term to co-accused—Syed Salman Saqib, Fahad Naseem and Sheikh Adil—in the Daniel Pearl abduction-cum-murder case. Omar Sheikh, a front ranking terrorist of the proscribed Jaish-e-Mohammed was prime the accused in the Pearl case. The court found Omar Sheikh guilty of committing offences under sections 7-A of the Anti-Terrorism Act, 365-A (kidnapping for ransom), 302 (murder) and section 120-A of the Pakistan Penal Code (conspiracy), after a trial inside the central prison. The judge sentenced the three co-accused to life imprisonment and a fine of Rs 500,000 each. The court also ordered that all the four accused to jointly pay an amount of Rs 2 million, which would be paid to Pearl's widow Mariane Pearl and their recently born son. The court held that Omar Sheikh was responsible for creating a sense of fear nationally and internationally and ruled that he had hatched a conspiracy and was the principal offender. The verdict said, Daniel Pearl being a captive of the accused stood proved and the non-fulfillment of their demands has presumably resulted in the murder of Pearl at the hands of the accused.

July 12, 2002: Pakistani authorities in Karachi arrested an alleged financial adviser of Osama bin Laden and two other terrorists believed to be from the Al Qaeda. Three Al Qaeda cadres, including Sheikh Ahmed Saleem, who was reportedly acting as a financial adviser of bin Laden in Pakistan, were arrested during an overnight raid on a suburban apartment in Karachi. Saleem, a Sudanese, reportedly escaped from Afghanistan to Pakistan after the US-led military campaign began in October 2001, said official sources.

July 7, 2002: Eleven Al Qaeda suspects were arrested from the Clifton area and Shah Noorani area of Baluchistan. Security forces recovered 57 weapons from their possession, including rocket launchers, light machine guns, Kalashnikovs, satellite telephone instruments, letters of Osama Bin Laden and Taliban chief Mullah Mohammed Omar. The arrested suspects include an Egyptian and an Afghan national, as also five cadres of the outlawed Sipah-e-Mohammed Pakistan.

July 3, 2002: Four Al Qaeda terrorists and two security force personnel were killed and two police personnel injured in an encounter near Jarma bridge in Kohat. The four Al Qaeda cadres of Chechen origin were coming from the tribal area of Miranshah, headquarters of North Waziristan Agency, near the Afghan border. According to official sources, the Al Qaeda cadres were probably on a terrorist mission in Kohat or Peshawar. SF personnel recovered four Kalashnikovs, one machine-gun, two pistols, 15 hand-grenades and a rocket launcher from the encounter site.

June 30, 2002: Pakistani authorities arrested a suspected Arab Al Qaeda terrorist in the tribal territory bordering Afghanistan.

June 26, 2002: Ten Pakistan security force personnel and two Chechen Al Qaeda cadres were killed in an encounter in South Waziristan Agency. SF personnel had raided Azam Warsak, a remote tribal area bordering Afghanistan, and arrested Al Qaeda terrorists hiding there. The operation followed reports that Al Qaeda terrorists had taken shelter in the house of Abdul Khaliq Sarkikhel Wazir, a resident of Kaza Paunga. The raid was reportedly based on tip-offs from US intelligence agents that 40 to 50 Al Qaeda fugitives from the March 2002-Operation Anaconda offensive in eastern Afghanistan were hiding in two buildings.

June 23, 2002: Two Arabic-speaking men, two Afghan nationals and a Pakistani were arrested in a raid on the Afghan Support Committee (ASC)—a non-governmental organisation in Pabbi, Peshawar. The ASC is a Kuwait-based group reportedly set up by Osama bin Laden. Senior ASC employee Hussein Halil of Jordan is still in custody after being arrested in Pabbi for suspected Al Qaeda links in the last week of May 2002. The US government had frozen the ASC's assets in January 2002 for alleged links with the Al Qaeda.

June 12, 2002: The French police claimed that they have arrested five persons, including two Pakistani nationals, in a raid in two suburbs of Paris for suspected links to the Al Qaeda. They are also reportedly linked to Markaz-Dawa-al-Irshad, parent organisation of the Lashkar-e-Toiba, and other terrorist groups operating in the Indian State of Jammu and Kashmir. All the five are being accused of having provided logistical support to Richard Reid, the British "shoe-bomber". Reid, on December 22, 2001, unsuccessfully attempted to blow up a bomb contained in his shoe inside an American Airlines flight to Miami that he had boarded at Roissy—Charles de Gaulle Airport outside Paris. The two Pakistanis were arrested from a discrete residence they maintained in a back alley in the suburb of

Evry, located south of Paris. The other three persons were arrested from Mantes-la—Jolie, an urban neighbourhood west of Paris, which in the past has reportedly been an important centre of Islamist fundamentalists.

June 17, 2002: Judicial authorities in France decided to place under detention a Pakistani national, Ghulam-Mustafa Rama, for allegedly having provided logistical support to Richard Reid, the British national who is known as the 'shoe-bomber', for having attempted to set off an explosive concealed in his shoe during a flight on December 22, 2001 to Miami. Rama, who is also the founder of the French branch of Markaz Dawa al-Irshad, was arrested by French police on June 12 at his home in Evry. On the same day, another unidentified Pakistani national and three Franco-Algerians were arrested. Police sources indicated that they are investigating the possibility of Rama playing an important role in providing recruits for terrorist operations in the Indian State of Jammu and Kashmir.

June 11, 2002: According to New York Times, Pakistan has arrested several US citizens linked to the Al Qaeda near the Afghanistan border, including a suspected associate of suspected 'dirty bomb' builder Jose Padilla. Padilla alias Abdullah al Muhajir was arrested on May 8 at Chicago's O'Hare Airport after US officials said he had reportedly held extensive meetings with top-Al Qaeda terrorist Abu Zubaydah about possibly detonating a conventional weapon to spew radiological material in the United States.

March 4, 2002: At least two of the seven persons killed by Macedonian police in a weekend clash were Pakistani nationals who fought in Afghanistan, said Interior Minister Ljube Boskovski. On March 2, Macedonian police shot dead in an ambush seven persons who were thought to be part of an international terror network targeting US, British and German interests in the Balkan country. "We have hints that say the two came from Pakistan and fought in Afghanistan...After their participation in Afghanistan, they were transferred to the Balkans, to countries neighbouring (Macedonia)", said Boskovski.

March 3, 2002: Director of the CIA, George J. Tenet, reportedly briefed President Bush on the accumulation of fresh evidence regarding Al Qaeda's nuclear ambition. Tenet reportedly told Bush that Pakistan's nuclear weapons programme was more deeply compromised than either government has acknowledged publicly. Pakistan arrested two former nuclear scientists, Sultan Bashiruddin Mahmood and Abdul Majid, on October 23, 2001, and interrogated them about contacts with bin Laden and his lieutenants. Pakistani officials maintain that the scientists did not pass important secrets to Al Qaeda, but they have not disclosed that Mahmood failed multiple polygraph examinations about his activities. Although Pakistani authorities concluded that the scientists violated a secrecy oath during trips into Taliban-controlled Afghanistan, the government decided they would not have been able to give away information necessary to build a bomb. Pakistani official sources were quoted as saying that Mahmood and Majid had confessed that the ISI had sanctioned their charity activities and meetings with the Taliban supremo Mohammed Omar. The CIA has given a list of six more nuclear scientists to the Pakistani government whom it wants to probe on suspicion of having links with the Al Qaeda or Ummah Tamir-e-Nau (Reconstruction of the Muslim Ummah) of Dr Sultan Bashiruddin Mahmud. The issue was also discussed between President Pervez Musharraf and CIA Director John Tenet during the latter's visit to Pakistan in December 2001. Two of the six scientists, Dr Suleiman Asad and Dr Muhammad Ali Mukhtar, are directly related to the country's nuclear programme, and have been working in the Kahuta Research Laboratories for the last few years.

November 13, 2001: Spanish authorities arrest ten persons suspected of having links to the international network of bin Laden. Interior Minister Mariano Rajoy was quoted as saying that the arrested were considered to be "the leading members of the Spanish infrastructure of the mujahideen movement…which forms part of the network of Osama bin Laden." Europa Press cited police officials as saying the detainees were responsible for the group's international relations and had held meetings in Pakistan, Yemen, the Philippines, Qatar and Afghanistan as well as in Europe.

September 29, 2001: Uganda's Joint Anti-Terrorism Taskforce arrest seven Pakistanis and a Zambian at Entebbe. The suspects—thought to be both drug traffickers and members of bin Laden's terror network—were en route from Rwanda to Europe, The Post, a daily in Lusaka, Zambia, reported on October 2. Circumstantial evidence pointed out that drug traffickers based in Afghanistan and Pakistan have established hubs in the predominately Muslim coastal city of Mombasa, Kenya, and in the two islands comprising Zanzibar, Tanzania, where hundreds of Pakistani nationals and their East African counterparts are arrested for drug smuggling each year, according to the United Nations and government agencies.

September 16, 2001: A government source in the Chinese territory of Macau said that police had arrested seven Pakistani nationals after finding documents apparently containing instructions to attack US targets there and in Hong Kong if there were a strike on Afghanistan. Macau government sources said that the men were arrested after US authorities provided names to security forces in Macau and Hong Kong of people to watch for following 9/11.

September 2001: Israeli security officials arrested 23 persons belonging to various Islamist groups. Officials said that a Gaza resident who was the cell leader was sent by Hamas to Pakistan in 1998 to study terror techniques with bin Laden's network.

December 2000: Khalil al-Deek, a Jordanian, allegedly a front ranking terrorist of the Muslim Brotherhood is arrested in Peshawar, near the Afghan border with Pakistan, and extradited to Jordan.

September 2000: Three Pakistani men were arrested in southern Philippines on suspicion they had been smuggling weapons to the Abu Sayyaf terrorist outfit. Quoting official sources, the Herald said, "since the Abu Sayyaf has been getting millions of dollars in ransom payments during the past five months they have gone on a weapons buying spree and we know that a lot of the weapons have come from Pakistan."

Year 2000: Israel arrested a Hamas cadre named Nabil Aukel who was trained in Pakistan and then moved to Afghanistan and Kashmir to put that training into practice.

December 1999: Some members of a terrorist cell are arrested in Jordan. The terror network was composed mostly of Jordanians of Palestinian origin, as well as an Iraqi, an Algerian and Palestinians with American passports. The detainees admitted during interrogation that they had been trained in Afghanistan in a training camp financed by bin Laden, and were assisted by contact members of Al Qaeda in Afghanistan and Pakistan. The group planned to carry out mass attacks against Jewish and American tourists and Christian pilgrims at the Radison hotel in Amman, at Mount Nevo, at the checkpoints on the Israeli-Jordanian borders, and at the place where Jesus was baptized. The central activists responsible for the logistics and religious authorization for the attacks were three Palestinians who operated from Afghanistan, Pakistan, and the UK.

June 1999: Eight persons of Pakistani origin are arrested in Yemen. Although they claimed that they had come for a holiday, security sources indicated that these men aged 17 to 33, were Islamist terrorists on a mission to kill fellow Britons. They were reportedly trained and armed in the mountains of Abyan by an obscure terrorist group called the Islamic Army of Aden (IAA), which wants Yemen to become an Islamic state. Ahmed Mohammed Hamed Ali, wanted in connection with the August 7, 1998, bombings of the United States Embassies in Dar es Salaam, Tanzania, and Nairobi, lived in Kenya until fleeing that country on August 2, 1998, to Karachi. Jamal Ahmed Fadl, 38, a one-time grocery store clerk from Sudan, and L'Houssaine Kherchtou, 37, a former catering student born in Morocco testifying before a 12-member federal jury in New York, investigating the 1998 embassy bombings, admitted to the existence of Al Qaeda's training at camps in Afghanistan, Pakistan and Sudan in firearms, explosives, computers, electronics, passport forgery and surveillance.

December 23, 1998: Seven men, including three Britons of Pakistani origin, are arrested in Yemen. The Yemeni government claimed they were carrying plans to blow up a church, a hotel and the British consulate.

July 1997: Two Palestinians and a Pakistani were arrested on a tip-off to New York City police and were found to have suicide bombs and a note indicating they intend a terrorist attack in the city's subways. Lafi Khalil, the Pakistani, entered the country on a tourist visa and stayed on illegally.

Year 1995: Abdul Hakim Murad, a Pakistani citizen, was arrested in Philippines following an abortive bomb explosion. Consequent to interrogation, Murad told the story of "Bojinka"—"loud bang"—the code name bin Laden operatives had given to an audacious plan to bomb 11 U.S. airliners simultaneously and fly an air plane into the CIA headquarters in Langley, Va.—all after attempting to assassinate Pope John Paul II. Investigators also found a stack of passports—Norwegian, Afghan, Saudi, Pakistani—from the apartment from which he was arrested. Codenamed "BOJINKA," the plot involved using a timing device made from an altered Databank watch. Flight schedules and a decrypted letter found on the computer indicated that five participants were to simultaneously plant devices on flights to the United States. After the bombings, four of the participants were to return to Karachi, Pakistan. The fifth was to return to Doha, Qatar. Jamaat-ul-Fuqra (JuF), a terrorist outfit operating in Pakistan and North America, was formed by a Pakistani cleric, Sheikh Mubarak Ali Gilani, in the early 1980s. In the 1980s, they carried out various terrorist activities, including murders and fire-bombings, across the United States. Although Gilani, the chief of Fuqra resides in Pakistan, most of his group's cells are located in North America. JuF is allegedly linked through court documents to 'Muslims of Americas', a tax-exempt group established in the United States in 1980 by Gilani, who was taken into Pakistani custody in connection with the abduction of murdered US journalist Daniel Pearl. ·Although dormant in terms of real activity, it has an active link with terrorist groups in Pakistan and provides both moral and material assistance to these groups. South East Asia The Moro Islamic Liberation Front (MILF) dispatched a first group of trainees to Pakistan in 1980. Most traveled with travel documents acquired after receiving false employment with a Middle East firm. The MILF has ex-filtrated its cadres out of the Philippines and into Pakistani and Afghan training camps. The MILF chairman Salamat Hashmi spent considerable time in Pakistan and knew many of the leaders of the Arab brigades of the Mujahideen. The origins of Abu Sayyaf Group (ASG) can be traced to Afghanistan. In the early-1980's approximately 200 Moro fundamentalists arrived in Peshawar to serve with the Mujahideen. One of them, Ustadz Abdurajak Janjalani emerged as their leader. It is in Peshawar that Janjalani befriended bin Laden. He also developed a close association with Ramzi Yousef, mastermind of the 1993 World Trade Centre bombing. Laden was looking to expand his global network and Janjalani was looking for money to strengthen his movement and Yousef was looking for a new mission. Everything came together in Peshawar in 1991. Following the Soviet withdrawal from Afghanistan, he began making frequent trips between his home in Basilan and the Peshawar-Afghan border region recruiting supporters. Ramzi Yousef moved to Manila in September 1994 to begin planning a second round of attacks on American targets. While in Philippines, he established a compartmenatlised cell of approximately 20 persons. Key cell members included Wali Khan Amin Shah, a close associate of Yousef. Amin Shah was born on the Pakistani-Afghan border. He previously worked for the Saudi-based Islamic International Relief Organisation (IIRO) in Peshawar (Pakistan). He is reported to have been the over-all charge of the financial logistics of the cell. On December 15, 1994, he was issued a three-month visa for Malaysia from the Malaysian embassy in Pakistan, indicating that he may have intended to seek a safe haven in Malaysia after the Pope's assassination. Another of the important members of the Yousef cell was Abdul Hakim Ali Hasmid Murad, a Pakistani national. He had first come to the Philippines between November 1990 and February 1991. Ramzi Yousef trained him in Lahore in August 1994 in bomb making. Murad was also a trained commercial pilot. Munir Ibrahim, another cell member hailing from Saudi Arabia had met Wali Khan Amin Shah in 1992 in Karachi. Amein Mohammed was another Pakistani national part of the Yousef cell and had established a firm in Malaysia, Konsojaya SDN, BHD. Yousef and Wali Khan Amin Shah established a shell company, the Bermuda Trading Company, as a cover to purchase chemicals.

December 10, 1994: A Philippines Airlines 747–200 flight 434, carrying 273 passengers and 20 crew, en route from Cebu to Tokyo was forced to make an emergency landing after a bomb went off in the cabin, killing a Japanese businessman. Later, Yousef called and claimed responsibility for the bombing in the name of the ASG. This bombing, though claimed to be the work of the ASG, was a dry run to test Yousef's plan to bomb 11 US jet-liners in "48 hours of terror". Fathur Rohman al-Ghozi aka abu Saad, an Indonesian national arrested on January 15, 2002, is linked to the Al Qaeda network. Al-Ghozi had been living in Philippines since 1996–97, where he came after studying in a madrassa on the Pakistan-Afghan border. Reports indicate that he was supposed to liaise with the MILF. As of December 2001, there were an estimated 200 undocumented Filipinos in Afghanistan and 600 'Islamic scholars' of Filipino origin in Pakistan. Of those in Pakistan, some 200 are 'missing' according to the Philippine Embassy at Islamabad. According to Malaysian academic Farish Noor, who studies the growth of Islamicism in Malaysia, "I've visited a school in Peshawar (Pakistan) that was officially listed as having three Malaysian students. In one class there were 50." He is estimated that some 300 students return annually after such 'education' in Pakistan. Parti Islam SeMalaysia, (PAS) suffered a serious blow when 10 cadres of the Kampulan Mujahideen (seven of whom were also PAS members) were detained on August 4, 2001 for attempting to violently overthrow the Malaysian regime and establish an Islamic state. Most of the members arrested had spent time with Tablighi Jamat in Pakistan. Riduan Isamuddin alias Hambali, a long time Al Qaeda operative and accused in Bali bombings, was a close associate of Ramzi Yousef and Wali Khan Amin Shah. He is known to have sent large number of young radicals to Pakistan and Afghanistan. In October 2001, two foreigners arrived in Singapore to assist in the planning of a series of attacks on US, British, Australian and Israeli diplomatic, military and commercial interests. One of them was a Pakistani named Muhammad Aslam Yar Ali Khan alias Sammy. He abruptly left Singapore for Pakistan on October 4, 2001, and has remained at large there (unconfirmed). The Maktab al Khidimat Lilmujajidin al Arab (MAK), founded by Abdullah Yousuf Azzam, Palestinian Hamas leader, connects to Saudi Arabia and Pakistan. Installed in Peshawar, placed under the direct protection of the ISI, the MAK was basically supported, financed and controlled through Saudi Arabia. Indonesian media has reported that a Pakistani citizen identified as Havis Muhammad Saad Iqbal was deported to Egypt at that government's request on January 11, 2002, in connection with suspected terrorist activities. Iqbal is suspected of involvement in the 'shoe bomb' attempt by Richard Reid on the American Airlines jet en route from Paris to Miami, and other terrorist activities in Egypt, Indonesian daily Suara Pembaruan quoted Mahmud Hendropriyono, chief of the National Intelligence Agency, as saying. Pakistani support has been extended to the Moro Islamic Liberation Front (MILF)—a number of MILF leaders and members have lived in Pakistan and claim to have offices there. Abdul Sahrin, the 'intelligence chief' of Moro national Liberation Front (MNLF) was sent to various training camps in Pakistan. The National Islamic Command Council (NICC), a breakaway MNLF group headed by Melham Alam, is reported to have received financial support from Pakistan. When Ramzi Yousef was arrested in Pakistan, the FBI said they uncovered his plan to assassinate the then Philippine President Fidel Ramos in retaliation for the arrest of Abdul Hakim Murad and Wali Khan Amin Shah in Manila. Official sources in Philippines have said that the ASG was receiving funds from among others the League of Pakistani Islamic Propagation. Three foreigners tagged as members of an international extremist group were arrested in the Philippines in November 2001. Two Palestinians with Iraqi and Lebanese passports respectively and a Jordanian were reportedly responsible for the recruitment of southern Philippines-based rebels for terrorist training in Afghanistan, Pakistan and Iraq.

It's astonishing that, instead of all the above mentioned facts about Pakistan's involvement in international terrorist activities, USA still appreciates General Pervez Musharraf for his selective approach against terrorism. Moreover, it's impossible for any one to smuggle even a small peace of iron or paper from Kahota Nuclear facility in Pakistan without the knowledge and permission of ISI and Pakistan Army. In such a situation how General Pervez Musharraf made Abdul Qadir Khan as a scapegoat for nuclear proliferation by sparing ISI and Pakistan Army? This is indeed a glaring reflection of Fascism in the character of General Pervez Musharraf.

PAKISTAN'S INVOLVEMENT IN GLOBAL DRUG TRADE

Pakistan's involvement in Global Drug Trade was first sponsored by General Zia-ul-Haq when he had established a special unit within Inter-Services Intelligence (ISI) named as **The Joint Drug Control and Surveillance Unit (JDCSU)** which was made responsible to monitor poppy cultivation in different parts of Pakistan and Afghanistan undertaken for raising funds for further expansion of military strength and funding of Jihadi groups in Afghanistan and Kashmir. This special unit was under direct control of General Zia himself while he was assisted by General Akhtar Abdur Rehman. As said earlier, this special unit was formed in order to handle matters concerning poppy cultivation in different areas of Pakistan and Afghanistan. This unit performed the following functions:

1. **PROVISION OF OPIUM SEEDS** to the farmers which were imported from an American supplier based in Minnesota whose annual sales of seeds is around $100 Million+;

2. **PAYMENT OF SALARIES** to all farmers engaged in the poppy cultivation under the supervision of ISI & Pakistan military and Afghan drug lords;

3. **PROTECTION** of such farmers and their families from any threat of murder by fellow farmers or anti-drug agencies operating in Pakistan and Afghanistan;

4. **STORAGE FACILITIES** at Government godowns as part of proper pre-export arrangements

5. **INTERNATIONAL SMUGGLING** through Pakistan Air Force planes to Europe and USA

6. **CROSS BORDER TRANSPORTATION** to China, India, Nepal, Bhutan, Iran and Central Asian states

7. **SALE TO ARABS** in order to collect hard cash in USA Dollars

8. **SALE TO NORTH KOREANS** for them to organize their own funding through onward retail sales network in East Asian countries

According to BBC News report of 2nd September 2006, The UN Office on Drugs and Crime has predicted a 6,100-tonne harvest of opium in Afghanistan. Although, the US is the main backer of a huge drive to rid Afghanistan of opium, yet, the involvement of USA in supporting Pakistan's endeavour to promote poppy cultivation in different parts of Pakistan and Afghanistan cannot be ruled out. A top US drugs official recently warned that Afghanistan could be "taken down by this whole drug problem". The $2.7bn drugs trade accounts for about a third of Afghanistan's economy. In my opinion, such a grand trade cannot be handled single-handedly by the illitrate Afghan drug-lords. Definitely, it is Pakistan's ISI and Punjab's cruel and criminal military dictatorship which is fully involved in facilitation of international drug smuggling. The Vienna-based Office on Drugs and Crime said in its report that poppy cultivation in Helmand province (Afghanistan) alone, which has seen a sharp rise in Taliban-led attacks on international troops, had risen by 162% since last year. Only six of Afghanistan's 34 provinces are opium-free, the report says. Office chief Antonio Maria Costa said after presenting his report to Afghan President Hamid Karzai: "These are very alarming numbers. Afghanistan is increasingly hooked on its own drug." "Public opinion is increasingly frustrated by the fact that opium cultivation in Afghanistan is out of control," Mr Costa said. "The political, military and economic investments by coalition countries are not having much visible impact on drug cultivation."

Who will tell to Mr. Costa that Pakistan is 100% sponsoring the poppy cultivation. If at all Mr. Costa is aware of this glaring fact, why has he decided to refrain from reporting this crime in his report?

Afghanistan is the world's largest opium producer, providing almost three-quarters of global opium production. Recent trends indicate that poppy cultivation is spreading further into remote areas. Around 1.7 million people, 7 per cent of the population, are directly involved in poppy production.

Poppy is only produced on approximately 1 per cent of the total arable land in Afghanistan. The bulk of poppy production takes place on irrigated land. The province of Nangarhar is currently the largest poppy cultivating area. Whereas the majority of Afghan farmers cultivate opium poppy for reasons of poverty and lack of viable alternative incomes, most of the profits remain with national and international drug traffickers.

Opium as a product is attractive to farmers because it is durable and easy to store and carry to the market. Opium markets operate like spot and future markets, with traders providing credit to farmers for future production. According to UNODC estimates, almost 500,000 people are globally involved in the Afghan opium trade. With an average price for raw opium now at $300 per kilogram and expected yields of up to 40 kilograms per hectare, poppy cultivation is much more profitable for farmers than the production of other commodities. In 2005, poppy cultivation generated a gross income of around $1.50 billion, around $3,900 per opium-growing family. This compares to an average national wage of $2 per day.

Opium poppy plants (Papaver somniferum seeds) grow throughout the United States, Canada, and other parts of the world. They are featured in numerous gardening magazines, dried flower shops, and floral wholesalers. The seeds are used in the United States and especially Eastern Europe for culinary purposes (cooking). Even though possession of poppy seeds appears to be legal in the United States it is illegal to produce opium and may be illegal to grow poppies in USA. However, there being no law in USA which could ban exports of opium seeds to other countries, the real benefit of such negligence has been enjoyed by countries like Pakistan and Afghanistan which are major contributors to the global drug trade.

Pakistan has also been a producer of opium for exports and traditional domestic consumption since the time of Muslim rule and the British Empire. In 1979, however, as part of a pre-planned drama of PRETENCE played by the Military dictatorship of General Zia, the government of Pakistan responded to the problem of increased illicit opium production and trade by the enforcement of the Hadd Ordinance (an Islamic law concerning crimes). The ordinance brought existing law into line with Islamic injunctions which prohibited trafficking, financing or possession of more than 10 grams of heroin or one kg of opium. All poppy cultivation [licit and illicit] was banned and all government-controlled processing plants and retail outlets for licit opium were closed. However, this was only an attempt to show to the world that the government was keen to clean the mess of drug trade within the jurisdiction of Pakistan while the reality was much different. The drug trade was rather "NATIONALIZED" by the Zia regime whereby the drug trade came into direct control of Inter-Services Intelligence (ISI) and Pakistan Army.

In order to misguide the international community, Pakistan released an analysis of poppy harvesting trends at the national level which revealed a decline in the amount harvested from 9,441 hectares in 1992 to less than 284 hectares in 1999. Of the three main poppy growing areas, Dir district in north of Frontier province where the United Nations Drug Control Programme [UNDCP] has been active since 1985, accounted for approximately 60 percent of the opium harvested in the country. Over this period, the UNDCP spent 35 million US dollars on alternative development projects in Dir district. Alternative development interventions coupled with demonstrated government commitment led to a decrease in opium cultivation in Dir district from 3,500 hectares in 1992 to near zero in 2000, making Pakistan one of the most successful story as far as war on drugs was concerned. But, all this was not more than a false story.

The said false story short-lived as RECORD LAND WAS BROUGHT under poppy cultivation in Pakistan's Balochistan province in general and the North West Frontier Province in particular in 2002 breaking the 1998 figures of 950 hectares, which were the highest in the last five years.

The illicit crop has been cultivated on a total of 3,000 hectares of land in the Frontier province, bordering Afghanistan in the west, while in Balochistan province also bordering Afghanistan and Iran, it has been cultivated on 2,000 hectares of land, according to figures released by the Pakistan government to the United Nations Drug Control Programme (UNDCP).

The poppy crop is either ready to be harvested or has already been harvested in some parts of the growing areas. The UNDCP sources say the law-enforcement agencies could destroy not more than "one-third" of the total standing crop in the NWFP until the first week of May. Meanwhile, the paramilitary force—Frontier Corps—claims it has destroyed the entire crop in Balochistan which is a blatant lie.

The FC claim, however, has drawn a question mark. The FC told the UNDCP it had destroyed the entire crop. However, armed resistance in Balochistan was much higher than in the NWFP, particularly in the Gulistan area where the paras had a standoff with armed tribesmen using RPGs (rocket-propelled grenade launchers) and other small arms and light weapons to prevent paramilitary force from destroying their crop. Thomas Zeindl-Cronin, the UNDCP officer-in-charge in Islamabad confirmed that as a matter of policy he could not challenge the FC claim.

The paramilitary force operation against poppy in Balochistan's Gulistan, Chaman in Qilla Abdullah district, Zhob, Barkhan and Khuzdar areas lasted for about 14 days. Some people do claim that the authorities in Balochistan province left poppy cultivated on some influential people's lands untouched.

The Khyber Agency tribal zone, bordering Afghanistan the in North West Frontier Province, has witnessed poppy cultivation on 868 hectares of land while the Kurrum Agency, also at the border with Afghanistan, cultivated poppy on 812 hectares of land. The Home and Tribal Affairs Department in Peshawar expressed inability to destroy the crop in Khyber Agency because of "inaccessible terrain."

Prime reason for unusually high acreage for poppy this year behind temptation among farmers to bring vast land under poppy cultivation was the pre-season high price of poppy per kilogram by the buyers. The pre-season price of per kilo poppy was reported around $900. The socalled Anti-drug enforcement agencies say the international drug mafia hiked up the price to induce more farmers into poppy cultivation. Interestingly, once a bumper crop is ensured, the buyers drop the price to more than half the original price knowing the growers will have little option but to sell the crop at the end of the season. According to anti-drug NGO in Peshawar, price of a kilo of old stock opium in Pakistan was recorded at US$620 while in Afghanistan the price of old stock per kilo was US$586 in the beginning of this year. The price, according to buyers, has gone down further in recent weeks.

In line with its mandate, the special drug unit of ISI provided the farmers with poppy seeds and also cash money to maximize chances of good production this year. However, extremist religious groups' emergence as a strong political force in the wake of 2007 general elections in Pakistan can also regarded as one of the reasons behind the re-emergence of poppy cultivation since ISI is backing certain Wahabi groups within the Opposition parites. The Islamic groups, which used to call poppy crop as a "weapon" to use against the United States, did not denounce poppy cultivation, rather backed farmers to grow poppy with fullest cooperation and support of Inter-Services Intelligence (ISI).

In order to remove any doubts among the farmers, ISI also facilitated issuance of a religious decree (Fatwa) with the courtesy of a radical Wahabi Islamic party Jamiat Ulema-e-Islam (Fazlur Rehman group) whereby poppy cultivation was declared "Islamic." The infamous religious cult called Tablighi Jamat has no objection on use of drugs by the participants from NWFP in order to persuade them to continue taking part in "religious activities" of Tablighi Jamat.

The Muttahida Majlis-e-Amal or United Action Council, a conglomerate of six Islamic parties, legislators in the state assembly in North West Frontier Province have also backed farmers' bid in the Kohistan district to grow poppy. The district, which is on main Silk Route linking Pakistan with China, has seen poppy fields for the first time. The government launched no operation yet and it was dependent on the MMA legislators' help and support to negotiate destruction of poppy with growers. That appears coming slowly, I mean the legislators' support to the government.

Malik Faiz Muhammad Khan of Dogram, an influential chieftain of both Sultankhel and Paindakhel tribes in Upper Dir district and also an active member of radical Islamic Jamat-e-Islami party recently confirmed defending the growers. How can it be possible for an ordinary politician from a deprived province like NWFP to openly talk of poppy cultivation without moral support of Inter-Services Intelligence (ISI)? He further said that his people would continue to grow poppy unless the government helped them financially. Growing anti-US feelings promoted by ISI also seem to have contributed to the increase in land under poppy cultivation. North and South Waziristan agencies, two tribal zones bordering Afghanistan, have witnessed poppy cultivation for the first time. The people in the two zones are very conservatives and have strong anti-American feelings and sympathies towards the Taliban.

One Mr. Jehanzeb Khan who is Chief of Whari called upon the Muslims to use drugs as a "nuclear bomb" against the US "since USA attacks only the Muslim" countries. "Many people think the Muslim world can use drugs as a weapon against the United States". This propaganda reflects the presence of ISI behind such statements.

A former member of a county in Dir district, Humayun Khan advocate, said that the clerics "did not oppose poppy cultivation." Other different political parties also used the poppy issue to gain political points. He recalled that the Jamaat-e-Islami in the past used to describe poppy as a "weapon" against the United States and its belief seems unchanged.

The UNDCP spent 35 million US dollars to make both Lower and Upper Dir districts poppy-free through the Dir District Development Project (DDDP) from 1986–87 to 1998. In 1998, the NWFP Chief Minister Mehtab Ahmed Khan Abbasi sanctioned US$4.655 million when the UNDCP stopped the grant.

Mr Khan and other farmers alleged "very little money" out of the 35 million US dollars and $4.655 million was spent on bettering the lot of the farmers. "No alternative source of income was provided or there would have been no poppy today," says Khan.

The US government is spending huge amount on efforts for poppy-free Pakistan. Narcotics Affairs Section [NAS] in the US Embassy in Islamabad believes Pakistan still needs years to make itself totally a poppy-free country. Experts at the NAS said unless communication facilities, mainly establishment of road networks, were provided in all the tribal zones poppy will be grown every year. The NAS helped the federal government construct 400 kilometres long roads in both Bajaur and Mohmand Tribal Zones. And because of road network law enforcing agencies were able to reach the area where poppy was grown and destroyed it.

But on the other hand, where there is no road network in a tribal zone, anti-poppy operations were not launched. The Pakistan government made no efforts to destroy standing crop in Khyber Agency tribal zone as it did not want to annoy the tribal people in the backdrop of underconstruction road network.

It is to be noted that since the demand for drugs has increased considerably, production is also rising. According to latest figures about drug addicts in Pakistan, there are a total of 4.1 million drug addicts, which is 2.8 percent of the total population of Pakistan. Among the 4.1 million addicts, the proportion of heroin addicts was two million, which is 50 percent of the total drug addicts. The number of drug addicts is on the rise in Pakistan. According to a survey in 1992, total drug addicts were 1.3 million. But they increased to 5.1 million in 2005 forecasting an alarming annual increase in the number of drug addicts. Among the drug addicts, 61% were literate, 54% were married, 26% were skilled workers, 25% were unskilled and 68% were labourers and sales personnel.

Pakistan cannot remain unaffected by political, social and economical environment in neighbouring Afghanistan. Poppy has been grown in areas that mostly border with Afghanistan. Whenever there are a leftists, nationalists or fundamentalist-led government in Kabul, similar political parties in the North West Frontier Province are also encouraged. The four-year Taliban rule in Afghanistan also resulted in strengthening of far-right Islamic groups in Pakistan's Frontier province. The province is ruled by the alliance that supported the Taliban regime against the US attack after the 9/11 terrorists attacks in the US. The same alliance is pursuing some policies for which the Taliban were known. So, the tribe that lives on Pakistan side also lives on the other side of the Durand Line, the international border between the two countries. Their religion, language, culture and traditions are more or less the same. They are inter-linked with each other. In due cooperation with Pakistan's Inter-Services Intelligence (ISI), almost all the successive governments in Kabul offered special incentives for tribal people living on Pakistan side. Since vast areas have been brought under poppy cultivation in Afghanistan, ISI exported "skilled labourers" from Pakistan this year to take care of the crop as Afghanistan was short of qualified labourers. Each labourer is being paid Rs.600 $12 a day, which is quite a big amount keeping in view low wages for labourers in Pakistan. Average wage a labourer gets in Pakistan is around Rs.300 ($5). When these labourers return home (Pakistan), they talk to their own people to suggest that growing poppy is several hundreds times profitable than going for other crops. So, they bring back with them inspiration and local people really get inspired. Secondly, officially it was said that one of the reasons behind increased poppy cultivation in Pakistan was involvement of Afghan nationals. The Afghans took land on lease to grow poppy in several areas particularly in tribal areas. So, much also depends as to what is happening in Afghanistan if we look at the drug problem in Pakistan. One can say each country suffers from the situation in its neighbouring country. On the contrary, the reality is that both Pakistan and Afghanistan are mutually involved in cultivation, storage, smuggling and promotion of poppy while international drug trade is also jointly sponsored by ISI from Pakistan and certain cabinet members of Karzai's government in Afghanistan.

If Pakistan is disintegrated, the network of poppy cultivation will also perish as a result of destruction of Inter-Services Intelligence (ISI) which is controlling and promoting poppy cultivation in different parts of Pakistan and Afghanistan.

REALITY OF 'TABLIGHI JAMAT' AND ITS MISSION

Tablighi Jamaat was formed by WAHABI Government of Saudi Arabia in order to spread their message in India. History is itself a great witness to this fact that certain Ulema (religious scholars) from Deoband (India) were invited by the then King of Saudi Arabia some 75 years ago. The then Saudi King offered to these characterless, greedy and selfish religious scholars money and support to launch a massive campaign to "combat" Shias in India. Hence, one Maulana Ilyas (who is respected like a prophet in the circles of Tablighi Jamat) along with his other fellow scholars agreed to form a particular Jamaat (group) called Tablighi Jamat to follow a specified agenda of the Saudi Kingdom. Their job was defined to them and they were sent back to India with a programme approved by the then Saudi Kingdom. However, the penetration into Indian religious circles was not an easy job for these scholars of Deoband, hence, they decided to catch some poor villagers of a nearby village and offered them money and food if they had agreed to hear the sermons of these scholars in the mosque. This was the beginning of an era of an innovative brand of Islam commonly popularised as WAHABIAT on same principles and doctrine of WAHABIAT followed by the Saudi Kingdom though this Wahabiat was more nurtured in Indian colors.

Saudi Kingdom never stopped funding of Tablighi Jamaat till today. The most glaring evidence of this moral and financial support for Tablighi Jamaat is their acceptance on the British, American and Australian soils since the Saudi Kingdom assured these nations that Tablighi Jamaat was working on a specific agenda of combatting Shiaism and had nothing to do with propagating Islam or provoking Christianity or Judaism.

Tablighi Jamaat (Pakistan Chapter) was partnering with Inter-Services Intelligence (ISI) to assist the latter in producing 'fighters of Islam' during the Soviet invasion whereby Tablighi Jamaat sent thousands of its workers in the form of preaching groups in line with its normal function, in order to facilitate religious propaganda about holy war (Jihad) amongst the young and foolish Afghan as well as Pathan Muslims living in Afghanistan and Pakistan's North West Frontier Province (NWFP or Pakhtoonkhwa). This strategy was very successful as thousands of 'free lance fighters' were recruited to 'sacrifice' their lives for Islam at that time. This was indeed possible as a result of constant brain-washing conducted by several religious scholars of Tablighi Jamat who are paid by the Saudi Kingdom for these services since long. ISI being an organ of the Pakistan's military has always acted in accordance with the decisions taken by the top elite of Punjab's military dictatorship since its inception. Hence, when Saudi Kingdom was in need of an effective supply of manpower to facilitate international terrorism around the world with special focus on USA, UK and Australia, they approached Tablighi Jamaat to provide such trained and brainwashed 'fighters' who were ready to accept death in exchange of paradise. It has been a great privilege on the part of hypocrite scholars of Tablighi Jamat in extending service to the royal Saudi Kingdom since long as the inception of Tablighi Jamat was itself part of Saudi strategy to propagate WAHABIAT in India for combatting Shia Islam in the subcontinent.

It is also interesting to note that Tablighi Jammat has not even bothered to obtain "go-ahead" from learned Islamic scholars of India since Tablighi Jamaat is of the opinion that Saudi Kingdom which follows WAHABIAT as their brand of Islam is the only authority on this earth to legitimize the functions of Tablighi Jamaat.

Please see below Fatwa of Shaykh 'Abdul-'Azeez ibn Baaz regarding Tablighi Jamat:

Question: I went out with the Jamaa'ah at-Tableegh to India and Pakistan. We used to congregate and pray in masaajid within which there were graves and I heard that the salaah in a masjid within which there is a grave is invalid. What is your opinion of my salaah and should I repeat them? What is the ruling about going out with them to these places?

Response: Indeed, the Jamaa'ah at-Tableegh do not have real knowledge pertaining to issues of 'aqeedah so it is not permissible to go out with them except for the one who has real knowledge of the correct 'aqeedah of Ahlus-Sunnah wal-Jamaa'ah. In this, he can enlighten them, advise them and co-operate with them in good because they are active in their affairs. However, they are in need of more knowledge from those who can enlighten them amongst the scholars of Tawheed and Sunnah. May Allaah grant everyone understanding of the religion and firmness upon it.

As for the salaah in the masaajid within which are graves, then it is incorrect and it is obligatory upon you to repeat all that you did (in those masaajid) due to that which the Prophet (sal-Allaahu `alayhe wa sallam) said:

((Allaah has cursed the Jews and the Christians who have taken the graves of their Prophets' as places of worship))—it's authenticity is agreed upon.

Also, his (sal-Allaahu `alayhe wa sallam) statement:

((Indeed those before you used to take the graves of their Prophets' and pious people as places of worship, so do not take the graves as places of worship, for certainly I prohibit you from that)), transmitted by Muslim in his Saheeh.

And the ahaadeeth on this subject are numerous—and with Allaah lies all success and may Allaah send prayers upon our Prophet Muhammed, his family and his companions.

Another Fatwa:
Fatwa of the Shaykh Muhammed Naasiruddeen al-Albaanee regarding Tablighi Jamaat:

Question: What is your opinion concerning the Jamaa'ah at-Tableegh? Is it permissible for a student of knowledge or other than him to go out with them under the guise of inviting to (the path of) Allaah?

Response: The Jamaa'ah at-Tableegh (TJ)does not uphold the manhaj of the Book of Allaah and the Sunnah of His Messenger (sal-Allaahu `alayhe wa sallam) and that which our Pious Predecessors were upon.

And if the situation was such, then it is not permissible to go out with them because it defies our manhaj in calling to the manhaj of the Pious Predecessors. So in the path of inviting to Allaah, then an `aalim can go out with them but as for those (ignorant—without knowledge) who go out with them, then it is obligatory upon them to remain in their countries and (study Islaam) seek knowledge in their masaajid until there graduates from amongst them people of knowledge who hold study circles inviting to the path of Allaah.

As long as the situation is like that, it is upon the student of knowledge to invite these people (those from Jamaa'ah at-Tableegh) to study the Book of Allaah and the Sunnah and invite people to it.

And the Jamaa'ah at-Tableegh, with respect to da'wah to the Book and the Sunnah, do not intend by it a starting point, rather they consider that to be a divided call (da'wah)/approach; And because of this, they most resemble the Jamaa'ah of al-Ikhwaan al-Muslimeen.

They say their da'wah is based upon the Book of Allaah and the Sunnah, however this is mere idle talk for certainly they have no 'aqeedah upon which they are united (which unites them)—so you find some are Maatureedee, others are Ash'aree, whilst others are Soofee and even some who have no madhhab (affiliation to any particular ideology).

This is because their da'wah is built upon amassing (the people), then gathering together and culturising/instructing them, and in reality they do not really have any culture. More than half a century has passed and there has not appeared from amongst them a scholar.

As for us, then we say instruct them, then gather together, such that the gathering together is based upon a foundation in which there is no doubt.

So the da'wah of the Jamaa'ah at-Tableegh is that of the Soofiyyah, they call to good manners, as for correcting the differing 'aqeedah of the group, then they do not exert themselves one iota. This is because they believe this will cause differences (and splitting apart).

It came to pass that a brother, Sa'd al-Husayn had much correspondence with the leader of the Jamaa'ah at-Tableegh in India or Pakistan and it became clear from that they acknowledge (belief in) intercession and seeking help (from other than Allaah) and many other such things. And they require their people (members) to make bay'ah (oath of allegiance) based upon four issues: amongst them the Naqshbandiyyah methodology. So it is upon every tableeghee (one who ascribes to the Jamaa'ah at-Tableegh) to make bay'ah of these fundamentals (issues).

A questioner may ask: Indeed this group has corrected its faults (returned to Allaah) as a result of the efforts of many individuals and quite possibly many non-Muslims have accepted Islaam at their hands. Is this not sufficient (proof) for the permissibilty of going out with them and participating in that which they call to?

So we say: Indeed we know these words and hear them a lot and know them to emanate from the Soofiyyah! For example, there is a Shaykh whose 'aqeedah is incorrect and does not know anything about the Sunnah. Instead they deceitfully take from the wealth of the people, so together with this, many open sinners seek forgiveness from them!

So every group which invites to good, then it is imperative they should be in adherence (to the Qur.aan and the Sunnah), and (this) our approach is pure, so what are they (others) calling to?

Are they calling to adherence to the Book of Allaah and the Sunnah of the Messenger (sal-Allaahu 'alayhe wa sallam) and the;aqeedah of the Pious Predecessors, abandoning blind following of the madhhabs to such an extent that they adhere to the Sunnah over and above their madhhab!? So the Jamaa'ah at-Tableegh do not have a knowledge-based (manhaj), rather, their manhaj is according to the place where they are to be found, so they change their "colours" to suit themselves
(source: www.fatwa-online.com)

Now the role of Tablighi Jamaat has further expanded. On one hand, they are collecting funds from Saudi Kingdom for propagating a new brand of Islam (WAHABIAT) while on the other, they are sponsoring "brain-washing factories" to produce new minds who consider TERRORISM as legitimate and fully Quranic. This poisonous preaching of their brand of Islam has already begun damaging the very structure of Islam in the modern world.

Please have a look at some input from different sources about Tablighi Jamat:

A Muslim Missionary Group Draws New Scrutiny in U.S.

Author: Susan Sachs
Publication: The New York Times
Date: July 14, 2003

One of Al Qaeda's first assignments for Iyman Faris, the Ohio truck driver named last month in a terrorist plot to destroy the Brooklyn Bridge, was to visit a travel agency while he was in Pakistan in late 2001 to have some old airline tickets reissued, federal investigators say.

Because the tickets were not in his name, Mr. Faris needed an explanation to validate his request. Investigators say he used one that other Qaeda recruits have relied on to disguise their intentions: he pretended to be a member of Tablighi Jamaat, a fraternity of traveling Muslim preachers that is well known in Pakistan and other Muslim countries.

Founded in rural India 75 years ago, Tablighi Jamaat is one of the most widespread and conservative Islamic movements in the world. It describes itself as a nonpolitical, and nonviolent, group interested in nothing more than proselytizing and bringing wayward Muslims back to Islam.

But since the attacks of Sept. 11, 2001, Tablighi Jamaat, once little known outside Muslim countries, has increasingly attracted the interest of federal investigators, cropping up on the margins of at least four high-profile terrorism cases.

It has been cited either as part of a cover story like Mr. Faris's, or as a springboard into militancy, as in the case of John Walker Lindh, the American serving time for aiding the Taliban.

Law enforcement officials say the group has been caught up in such cases because of its global reach and reputation for rejecting such worldly activities as politics, precisely the qualities that are exploited by terror groups like Al Qaeda.

The name Tablighi Jamaat is Arabic for the "group that propagates the faith," and its members visit mosques and college campuses in small missionary bands, preaching a return to purist Islamic values and recruiting other Muslim men—often young men searching for identity—to join them for a few days or weeks on the road.

"We have a significant presence of Tablighi Jamaat in the United States, and we have found that Al Qaeda used them for recruiting, now and in the past," said Michael J. Heimbach, the deputy chief of the F.B.I.'s international terrorism section.

Another senior law enforcement official described the group as "a natural entree, a way of gathering people together with a common interest in Islam."

The official added, "Then extremists use that as an assessment tool to evaluate individuals with particular zealousness and interest in going beyond what's offered."

Neither the organization nor Tabligh activists have been accused of committing any crime or of supporting terrorism. Yet the authorities remain alert to what they see as the group's susceptibility to infiltration and manipulation.

To Tabligh leaders, accustomed to operating in relative obscurity, the new scrutiny is unwanted, and the government's contention that the group has served as a recruiting ground for terrorists is grossly unfair.

In interviews over the past several months, they said their beliefs were antithetical to everything espoused by Osama bin Laden and Al Qaeda.

A Renunciation of Politics

"It's a very great accusation, a total lie," said Abdul Rahman Khan, a leader of the group's North American leadership council. "Anybody who has been active in our work, who spends at least three days, will have an understanding of our peaceful nature."

Mr. Khan, who lives near New Orleans and has been involved with the group for 36 years, said the Tablighi Jamaat's refusal to discuss politics meant that people with militant views quickly moved on.

"From our experience, those people who have those intentions don't talk around us," he said. "If someone starts even one word, we cut him off. So he's going to go somewhere where he can get an audience."

Indeed, the number of core activists is quite small, and they do little to blend in. A gathering of American and Canadian Tablighi Jamaat missionaries this year drew about 200 people. It was at Al Falah mosque in Corona, Queens, a Tabligh center whose neighbors have grown accustomed to the sight of bearded men wearing robes and leather booties that are meant to replicate the dress of Islam's prophet, Muhammad.

Younger disciples who were not emirs, or leaders, of a region or city, remained outside, using the time to proselytize for Islam in the mostly Mexican immigrant neighborhood. Inside, their elders mulled the question of whether they should be held responsible for the actions of people who take part in Tabligh missions but are not dedicated to its beliefs.

"We don't prevent anyone from coming, but obviously we don't know the nature of the individual who is coming and we don't check," Mr. Khan said. "There's no way we can."

The Tablighi Jamaat is less a formal organization than a network of part-time preachers. Begun as a response to a surge of Hindu proselytizing during the waning days of British rule in India, the Tablighi Jamaat now has bases and schools in Pakistan, Britain and Canada. Its annual gatherings in India and Pakistan draw hundreds of thousands.

Traveling and Proselytizing

Generally, though, Tabligh missions are small—a few heavily bearded men, carrying sleeping bags and cooking stoves who show up at a mosque, give lectures and go door to door calling Muslims to prayer.

A central purpose of their visits is to ask other men to travel and preach with them for a time, which they say can benefit the preachers even more than their audiences.

"It's kind of a rite of passage for practicing young Muslims," said Mairaj Syed, a law student at U.C.L.A. who says he was briefly involved with the Tablighi Jamaat in high school in Arizona.

"They emphasized identity, showing outwardly that you are a Muslim," Mr. Syed said. "Also, there was the element of going out, visiting cities, sleeping in mosques. I thought it was cool."

They preach a return to the teachings and trappings of Islam's seventh-century founders, including segregation of women and rejection of activities like voting that they say distract Muslims from the worthier task of preparing for judgment day.

Their goals, the group's American leaders say, are devotion to God and promoting change in each individual, not society.

"What we're trying to do is unite the hearts of all people, and politics has a propensity to divide," said Walid-Muhammad Scott, a Philadelphia activist who is a member of the leadership council. "That's why we don't talk about it at all."

But law enforcement officials and moderate Muslim scholars say that disengagement from society is what worries them most about the Tablighi Jamaat.

"You teach people to exclude themselves, that they don't fit in, that the modern world is an aberration, an offense, some form of blasphemy," said Khaled Abou El Fadl, a professor of Islamic law at U.C.L.A. "By preparing people in this fashion, you are preparing them to be in a state of warfare against this world."

Ripe for Exploitation?

Professor El Fadl said he spoke from experience, having briefly joined the group as a teenager in Cairo about 20 years ago. "I don't believe there's a sinister plot where they're in bed with Osama bin Laden but are hiding it," Professor El Fadl said. "But I think that militants exploit the alienated and withdrawn social attitude created by the Tablighis by fishing in the Tablighi pond."

Some Muslim groups have long criticized the Tablighi Jamaat for its official refusal to take a stand on the causes that have inflamed the Muslim world, from the Afghan holy war against the Soviet Union in the 1980's to the more recent wars over Kashmir, Chechnya and Bosnia.

But investigators in America and elsewhere say more violent groups have been well served by the Tablighi Jamaat's apolitical stance and ability to move missionaries around countries and across borders.

"There may be groups that do not actually profess its basic ideology and profound religiosity and yet use the cover of the Tablighi Jamaat in order to evade scrutiny of the security forces, knowing full well that the Jamaat would not take a public stance against any defectors," the Canadian intelligence service said in a recent analysis.

A turning point for the movement came in the 1990's, with the emergence of the purist Islamic rule of the Taliban in Afghanistan, according to former members and intelligence officials.

By way of illustration, Farad Esack, a South African Islamic scholar who says he spent 12 years with the group in Pakistan, recounted a favorite Tablighi Jamaat analogy that equates individual Muslims to the electricians who work to light up a village. Each person lays wire until one day, the mayor comes to switch on the lights.

"For many people in Tablighi Jamaat," he said, "the Taliban represented God switching the lights on."

Some people drawn to the Tablighi Jamaat were also drawn to the Taliban, Mr. Esack said. The Tablighi Jamaat, he said, "attracts angry people—people who need absolutes, who can't stand the grayness of life." In turn, that mentality "lends itself to being recruited by a Taliban-type project."

John Walker Lindh's path to militancy began in California, where he met Tabligh missionaries in 1999 after converting to Islam. He joined them on a proselytizing tour but soon left them behind.

"John's experience of the Tablighi is that they are what they say they are," said George Harris, one of Mr. Lindh's lawyers. "They are apolitical. And he found that an extreme position that he didn't find particularly attractive. He wanted guidance as to political and spiritual issues."

Mr. Lindh's experience, however, did play a role in his odyssey toward Afghanistan.

One year after his Tablighi Jamaat mission, casting about for a place to study Islam, Mr. Lindh contacted one of his visiting Tabligh preachers, who enrolled him in a madrassa, or religious school, in Pakistan.

It was there, Mr. Lindh has said, that he became convinced that he should help the Taliban. He then signed up for a military training camp that ultimately sent him to fight American and Northern Alliance forces in Afghanistan. He was captured there and is now serving 20 years in federal prison, having pleaded guilty to charges of aiding the Taliban and carrying explosives.

Federal prosecutors have suggested that the Tablighi Jamaat was also seen as a springboard by at least one of the defendants in a Portland, Ore., terrorism case, in which six men and one woman are accused of plotting to fight with the Taliban and Al Qaeda against American forces.

The men tried to get to Afghanistan in the late fall of 2001, according to the indictment. Most came home after spending some time in China, but one defendant, Jeffrey Leon Battle, went on to Bangladesh.

Prosecutors said Mr. Battle's trip there was aimed at finding Tablighi Jamaat members who might help him get military training and join the Taliban. His trial and that of the other Portland defendants is scheduled for early January.

Six Yemeni-American men from Lackawanna, a Buffalo suburb, apparently told family and friends a similar story—that they were going to Pakistan in the spring of 2001 for religious training with the Tablighi Jamaat. But once in Pakistan, the men went on to take military training at a Qaeda camp in Afghanistan, investigators say.

The six have pleaded guilty to providing material support to Al Qaeda, or otherwise aiding a terrorist organization through their attendance at the camp.

Federal investigators said the young men, before their trip, had been instructed by a recruiter from Al Qaeda to feign an interest in Tablighi Jamaat to build a believable excuse for traveling to Pakistan for their supposed religious course, rather than to an Arab country where some of them would at least have spoken the language.

In the case of Mr. Faris, who has pleaded guilty to charges of providing support for Al Qaeda, court documents did not say whether it was he or his Qaeda handlers who had the idea of using Tablighi Jamaat as a cover to organize a trip to Yemen without arousing suspicion.

Elders and Acolytes

Al Falah mosque is the main Tablighi Jamaat outpost on the East Coast and often serves as a meeting place for activists from the group's 11 regional zones and 37 local areas. They come from as far away as Canada, California and Florida to the plain-fronted mosque, almost lost on a busy street dominated by Mexican restaurants, a Buddhist temple and a Jehovah's Witness hall.

During the national gathering earlier this year, the wives of some of the members met in an apartment near the mosque. They sat cross-legged in one small room while a Tabligh elder, refusing to sit in the same room with women, shouted a lecture to them from behind a closed door.

Meanwhile, three Tabligh acolytes huddled over coffee in a Mexican restaurant across the street.

As a man from Cleveland tried to persuade the waitress to become a Muslim, one of his companions, a 19-year-old from North Carolina, talked excitedly of his own conversion just weeks before.

Sprouting a small reddish beard and dressed in a long tunic and loose trousers, he said Tablighi Jamaat had rescued him from drugs. Now, he said, his name is Ali Abdullah and his dream is to study Islam in Pakistan.

"I want to be in a Muslim environment," he explained.

Was he also interested in political causes like Chechnya, Kashmir or the Palestinian-Israeli conflict?

"Man, I know I'd kill anybody who killed another Muslim," he blurted, rapping a quick drumbeat with his hand on the table.

His two companions glared at him. One kicked him sharply under the table.

"We respect all people," said the man from Cleveland, who gave his name as Abdulhakim. "Tablighi Jamaat taught me that you don't need to protest, that we respect the prophets of the Christians and Jews." Unquote.

My argument about Tablighi Jamat is much more explosive than what is generally believed or accepted by different agencies around the world. The reason is very obvious. I spent more than 5 years with Tablighi Jamat and had opportunity to meet and see the top TJ's scholars in Raiwind. These people are really more dangerous than Osama Bin Laden or any other known terrorist of today because they are technically involved with Inter-Services Intelligence (ISI) for implementing a new dimension of terrorism designed by ISI for the 21st century. In line with this newest goal and objectives, Tablighi Jamat is no longer just a preaching group. Tablighi Jamat has engaged itself in the 'war-on-infidels' who are (as per their own definition) Christians, Jews and Hindus.

Tablighi Jamat is special in its activities which are propagated as very holy since such activities (as they say) have been approved and recommended by Prophet of Islam Muhammad SA. In private meetings organized at various Tablighi centres in Pakistan situated within the premises of thousands of mosques, Tablighi Jamat claims that the Holy Prophet Muhammad SA is always present in Raiwind and also monitors the activities and functions of Tablighi Jamat. They also claim that Muhammad SA is the real leader of Tablighi Jamat while His instructions are followed by the rest of the religious scholars in organizing all international work of Tabligh. Similarly, the top decision-makers of Tablighi Jamat have a special team of 'DREAM WRITERS' whose duty is to create and fabricate new versions of different dreams about the Tablighi Jamat to prove its being a holy group on this earth being administered directly by the Holy Prophet Muhammad SA. These dream writers can well be regarded as Creative Directors who write false stories and dreams in which there are messages from the Holy Prophet about the greatness and superiority of Tablighi Jamat in this world. There are also messages about fighting the evil and infidels (generally referred to Christians and Jews). The concept is to propagate these false dreams among the preachers who are in millions in order to keep their faith about Tablighi Jamat intact and also to have a continuous supply of manpower from areas like NWFP and rural Punjab for the purpose of different events organized on regular basis.

My research reveals that Tablighi Jamat works on the principle of Hypnotism. It is true that hypnosis, with its long and chequered history in medicine and entertainment, is now receiving some new respect from neuroscientists. Tablighi Jamat is an innovative Cult Group disguised as a religious school of thought where Miracle is combined with Mystery and Authority. Tablighi Jamat applies coercive psychological techniques for making its listeners and followers do what is asked for in a manner prescribed by the chiefs of Tablighi Jamat. They normally start with motivation of routine time-spending in (as they term it) the path of Allah for 40 days or 4 months depending on the mental ability of the prospective follower at the time of such brain-washing session.

Similarly, the elderly and the very young are not excluded from Tablighi groups, as demonstrated by the visible membership of the Tablighi Jamat. However, persons between the ages of 18 and 30 are especially subject to 'recruitment' and 'motivation' for proper brain-washing. In order to understand the working strategy of Tablighi Jamat, it is essential to define the concept of brainwashing. As defined, brainwashing refers to intensive, forcible indoctrination, usually political or religious, aimed at destroying a person's basic convictions and attitudes and replacing them with an alternative set of fixed beliefs. The application of a concentrated means of persuasion, such as an advertising campaign (or say religious campaign) or repeated suggestion, in order to develop a specific belief or motivation is known as brainwashing.

Tablighi Jamat has developed several methods of brainwashing from its experience of half a century. The top scholars of TJ are busy day-and-night to explore innovative methods to educate minds of young Muslim generation (as said earlier between ages 18 to 30) so as to make them obedient to the teachings of Islam (of a specific brand) in such an aggressive manner that a slight distraction should not be tolerated. This is for this reason that 90% Taliban fighters are either belonging to the same sect of Islam called WAHABI or are convinced that the real Islam is the one sponsored and propagated by Tablighi Jamat. The reason for this acceptance is quite obvious for the sole reason that Tablighi Jamat has covered itself under a huge umbrella of religious divinity. When people listening to the sermons of the TJ's scholars always hear that Muhammad SA (the Holy Prophet) has his fullest support and appreciation for Tablighi Jamat, how can it be possible for the listeners to refrain from embracing any belief that leads them to accept the glory of Tablighi Jamat. The poisonous speeches by the TJ's scholars round the clock and throughout the year make it rather impossible for the poor listeners (who are 99% illitrate and unable to read or write) to afford any contradiction or questioning validity or applicability of anti-Christian or anti-Jews messages conveyed in such speeches. Consequently, crops of hatred-filled socalled *Jihadists* are produced in abundance. In my opinion and to the best of my knowledge and belief, Tablighi Jamat has played a pivotal role in the mental training of Taliban on the specific instructions of Inter-Services Intelligence (ISI) during the Afghan war. General Zia-ul-Haq was a great fan of Tablighi Jamat and it is on record that he had always attended the mega Tablighi congregations orgnanized every year in Raiwind-Pakistan. I am myself a physical witness when I had seen General Zia-ul-Haq and Mian Nawaz Sharif (the then Chief Minister of Punjab) in the year 1986 together landing at the Heliport of Raiwind to attend 'DUA' being the final session of prayers on the last day of Tablighi congregation of that year. I was on stage sitting beside Maulana Inam-ul-Hasan Kandhalvi (known as Hazratjee) who used to come from India to close the congregation on the final day by performing a General Prayer called 'DUA'. My presence on the stage proves the fact that I was very much involved with Tablighi Jamat, hence, having access to several indoor discussions and inside stories of Tablighi Jamat so much so that I was also very close to certain top TJ's scholars who later thrown me out due to their suspicion about my beliefs similar to those of Shias or Sunni Muslims in the matter of Hazrat Imam Hussain and his father Imam Ali AS. I mean, I was considered a shia spy. However, I did have opportunity to meet and talk with one Maulana Saeed Ahmed Khan who had been deported back to Pakistan by the Saudi Kingdom in late 80s. Tablighi Jamat regards Saeed Ahmed Khan as a very pious scholar who had several in-person "meetings" with Prophet of Islam Muhammad SA and that Saeed Ahmed Khan was getting "direct instructions" from Muhammad SA to run the affairs of Tablighi Jamat. I believe that Tablighi Jamat is based on falsehood and their task has always been to advocate a specific brand of Islam commonly known as WAHABIAT under an agreed agenda approved by the Saudi Kingdom long time ago.

Since 1999, as soon as General Pervez Musharraf captured the power through an solicited bloodless coup, Inter-Services Intelligence (ISI) changed its strategy and carried out detailed studies to launch a massive war against USA, Israel, UK and India under a revised and more explosive Action Plan. This Plan of Action was not only limited to normal espionage methods or generally accepted principles of espionage, rather, it was a more detailed plan to supersede all conventional methods adopted by ISI earlier during the Afghan war against the Soviet Union. The fundamental objectives of this Action Plan are as follows:

1. To penetrate into civic societies of USA, United Kingdom and Australia;

2. To establish linkage with Muslims living in USA, United Kingdom and Australia through a religious platform (specifically Tablighi Jamat) in order to attract such Muslims to come closer to 'Islam';

3. To organize meetings with Muslim youth settled in USA, UK and Australia to make them aware of Quranic verses concerned with preaching (and fighting if necessary) in the path of Allah (God);

4. To promote and spread printed literature on the subject of Islam's (rather WAHABIAT's) rulings on issues concerned with formation of a just society by invoking Muslim laws (commonly known as Shariat) only for those who may ask for books (otherwise it was not necessary to depend on written materials but vocal brainwashing);

5. To liaise with other countries where Muslim population's representatives expressed readiness and willingness to welcome the idea of 'Islamization' in their societies; (Nigeria, Somalia and Sudan were selected as target countries)

6. To invite new crop of young Muslims from different Muslim countries (about 1000 to 3000) to Pakistan under the pretext of religious education, spending time in the path of Allah and understanding teachings of Islam in practical terms for replication in their respective countries;

7. To prepare a team of young, energetic and potentially capable young Muslims who should be educated, learned and able to follow professional guidelines by ISI;

8. To exchange communication with Islamist (Wahabi) orgnizations based in Egypt, Jordan, Syria and Iraq in order to keep a consistent check on the activities undertaken by such religious Tablighi (preaching) groups in their respective countries;

9. To collect statistics from different parts of the world concerning schools teaching aircraft flying courses and institutions offering courses on becoming a pilot;

10. To train a certain number of skilled (faithful, God-fearing and heaven-loving) young Muslims who have agreed for voluntary compliance to participate in JIHAD (holy war) as soon as instructions from Muhammad SA arrive via Tablighi Jamat;

In line with the implementation of above tasks set by ISI, the most efficient group assisting ISI is Tablighi Jamat. On one hand, ISI has a face of friendship with Americans and Englishmen being their partners in War-on-Terror while on the other, ISI is fully committed to organize all possible schemes to destroy Christians, Jews and Hindus from the world globe. In my opinion, the important thing is not what is being offered by the Pakistan's hypocrite military dictatorship to the West in War-on-Terror but what exactly is Pakistan's military dictatorship's hidden agenda. Obviously, I dont think that Americans or Europeans are cunning enough to judge the depth of conspiracy or conspiracies being developed by ISI to facilitate a new strategic plan to crush Christians, Jews and Hindus in the next 15–20 years through a holy war commonly known as *Jihad* which is already invoked in certain parts of Muslim world. ISI has, within its army of several thousand officers and workers, a long list of sympathisers and supporters of Islamic militant movements which have firm belief in aggression and destruction.

Tablighi Jamat is running an internal system whereby consent or agreement with a certain theoretical orientation is fully engineered. What can be termed the engineering of consent threatens all basic knowledge and action levels, undermining the right to withdraw consent and leave. Agreement is extracted through ethical pressure developed in an artificial spiritual environment, the right to question leaders is withheld, alternative sources of information are absent or ridiculed and people are systematically pressurised into escalating their level of involvement through quotation of Quranic verses concerned with fighting with 'Infidels' (Christians, Jews, Hindus etc as interpreted). Tablighi Jamat has a specific system in place which facilitates 'mind control'. This 'mind control' operates by taking such aspects of social influence and exaggerating them to the extent that people's thoughts, feelings and behaviour are manipulated to the greater gain of the manipulator, at the expense of the person being influenced. Such human interaction then consists of attempts to influence the cognitions and behaviour of others, while interaction within Tablighi Jamat is inherently inclined to encourage the development of shared norms and behaviours by the followers of this vicious Islamic cult group. However, since Tablighi Jamat has successfully closed down choice, restricted information flow, discouraged the expression of dissent, exaggerated its followers' sense of commitment by extracting public statements of loyalty (often after participation in religious meetings and congregations) and dominate the normal thinking process of affected individuals. In my personal opinion, the communication techniques of Tablighi Jamat's characterless, selfish and off-the-track scholars are as follows:

Reliance on the use-and abuse-of Quranic Verses:

On deceptive and distorted interpretation of several Quranic verses, artfully designed suggestion and intense emotional experience, crippling tactics aggravated by physical exhaustion and isolation on the part of socalled senior Tablighi workers help Tablighi Jamat to brainwash its followers in a systematic manner.

Similarly, lies or even "being economical with the truth" appear designed to recruit people through a process of *extracting commitment and then forcing a decision.* For example, Tablighi Jamat declares its followers and workers as legal owners of the Paradise. They tell openly in their 'sermons' that those who spend their time at Raiwind-Pakistan with the Tablighi Jamat earn such a huge reward from

God that even Angel Gabriel is unable to know about such rewards. As part of strategy, full extent of the Tablighi Jamat's organisation and programme is not immediately made clear to the new comers. Nevertheless, a commitment to some form of counselling activity is obtained, and sounds on first hearing much more acceptable than joining a holy war (Jihad) to save the world from the 'infidels'. A person is likely to imagine that they have delayed a decision to make such a total commitment, perhaps indefinitely. However, they soon find their initial levels of activity rising: "come to one more religious meeting at the local mosque," "attend one more Tablighi Ijtimah (Preaching Congregation)," "read relevant verses of Quran to understand the truth about Christians, Jews and Hindus."

Whether they have consciously decided anything becomes irrelevant:

After a thorough interaction with the socalled senior Tablighi workers, a real commitment is made to the Tablighi Jamat by new comers who then find that their attitudes are changing to come in line with escalating levels of commitment, and would eventually reach such an intense pitch that a formal decision (if it needs to be made at all) is only a small final step—a classic demonstration of cognitive dissonance theory. The manipulation of this process is, of course, a hallmark of salesmanship by Tablighi Jamat in general, whether the products include even global salvation.

Following are the main/salient characteristics which can be construed as mechanisms for engineering consent within Tablighi Jamat:

1. Charismatic leader figure, with authoritarian and narcissistic tendencies:

One man called Abdul Wahab along with other socalled scholars like Mufti Zainul Abedin, Moulvi Farooq, Moulvi Jamshed, Moulvi Muhammad Ahmed etc. etc. are known by all the members/workers of Tablighi Jamat as not-less-than any apostle of God on the earth. An artificial impression is given to all the Tablighi workers through false stories of miracles and dreams that the people running the Tablighi Jamat are God-fearing and beloved servants of God.

2. Idealising of leader by followers:

Frequently these false spiritual Tablighi scholars are hailed as a 'genius' or 'Men of God' and once it is done, it becomes very simple to make people do what is asked for…even to go in the path of Allah (God) and crush the Christians, Jews, Hindus and other infidels from this earth.

3. Followers regard their belief system as superior:

The brainwashing conducted by Tablighi Jamat compel its followers to regard their belief system as very superior to all others, and a more rational investigation of alternatives or the empirical verification of key concepts are fully discouraged and declared as 'infidelity'.

4. Becoming suspicious of other religions:

Links with others are discouraged, ensuring that ideas which do not originate within the Tablighi Jamat are 'translated' for the followers' benefit by leader figure. Taking advantage of such a situation, such Tablighi brainwashers tell false commandments about killing of Christians, Jews and Hindus.

In my opinion, goals set by the West to combat terrorism are not properly worked out. They think that Pakistan is their friend while Iran and Syria are their enemies. Dont forget that Pakistan's military dictatorship is predominantly comprised of Wahabi Islam sponsored by Saudi Kingdom through a perfect link of Tablighi Jamat. This link does not consider peace as a solution but insists on carrying out attacks on others in order to fulfil the obligations specified in the Quranic verses mentioned above. Tablighi Jamat is headed by the same brutal Punjabi dictators who had once stabbed Bengalis, then Baluchis & Sindhis, then Pathans & Urdu speaking majority of Karachi and also innocent and illitrate poor Afghans who were converted into "Taliban" for fighting against Soviet Union.

TABLIGHI JAMAT'S SECRET PLANS TO FORM ISLAMIC REPUBLIC OF XINJIANG

During my days with Tablighi Jamat back in 1986, I was able to participate in various indoor meetings organized by the top spiritual leaders of Tablighi Jamat in order for them to hear the progress reports of different Tablighi teams which came back from foreign tours/missions. One of such teams was of Lt. General Javed Nasir whose Tablighi team had returned from China after spening some weeks in the "path of Allah". Abdul Wahab, the main leader of Tablighi Jamat asked several questions and got rhetoric answers from Javed Nasir in an "ALL IS WELL" style. This made Abdul Wahab very upset and he scolded Javed Nasir to explain properly what he really did in China apart from routine "mosque exercises". I guess, Javed Nasir could not understand the real interrogation by Abdul Wahab or may be Javed Nasir decided not to speak in front of youngsters like me to hear the "sacred secret" which he might have inside his heart. Anyway, later we came to know that Abdul Wahab was enquiring about the progress towards formation of Islamic Republic of Xinjiang since Abdul Wahab spoke a lot about Islamization of China by 2020 since, as he stated, China was next target of Islamization after Soviet Union. Abdul Wahab explained that thousands of Afghans "sacrificed" their lives for the sake of Islam and as such this sacrifice would remain "incomplete" unless the entire communist/socialist block is crushed into pieces. He pointed out that China deserved Islamization more than USSR.

I was totally surprised to learn about the adventurous ambitions of Tablighi Jamat being involved in "educating" and "brainwashing" Muslims of Xinjiang to establish a unique Islamic force to liberate their province from China and to form Islamic Republic of Xinjiang. I am 100% sure that Javed Nasir being an important officer of ISI at that time must be involved in spying for ISI with the ulterior motive of creating a particular armed pressure group to run a campaign for an independent Islamic state.

According to a recent publication on mosques in China, there are now 32,749 mosques in the entire People's Republic of China, with 23,000 in the province of Xinjiang alone. Hence, the work of Tablighi Jamat in Xinjiang province is not only restricted to make "good Muslims" but also to pave way for an independent state called Islamic Republic of Xinjiang. There has been an increased upsurge in Islamic expression in China, and many nationwide Islamic associations have been organized to coordinate inter-ethnic activities among Muslims under the sponsorship of Tablighi Jamat. Islamic literature can be found quite easily and there are currently some eight different translations of the Qur'an in the Chinese language as well as translations in Uygur and the other Turkic languages which are financed by Tablighi Jamat's different local religious groups under the auspices of Saudi Kingdom. I remember that once Abdul Wahab of Tablighi Jamat gave an argument, during his morning speech addressed to only a specific group of Tablighi Jamat's members, that if USA could form a Jewish state of Israel on the land of Palestine, why cant we (Muslims) form an Islamic state on the Chinese soil (in the province of Xinjiang). He also quoted certain Quranic verses concerning preaching of Islam in different ways including formation of Islamic kingdom through power and holy war (Jihad).

Members of Tablighi Jamat in Xinjiang province have gained a measure of toleration from other religious practices. In areas where Muslims are a majority, the breeding of pigs by non-Muslims is forbidden in deference to Islamic beliefs. Muslim communities are allowed separate cemeteries; Muslim couples may have their marriage consecrated by an imam; and Muslim workers are permitted holidays during major religious festivals. The members of Tablighi Jamat in Xinjiang have also been given almost unrestricted allowance to go for

Hajj to Mecca. Due to activities of Tablighi Jamat in recent years, China's Muslim population living in different parts of the country have also become active in the country's internal politics.

The Xinjiang Autonomous Uighur Region, located in China's northwest, is home to approximately eight million Uighur Muslims. There are several million Hui, Kazakh, and Tajik Muslims as well. Province of Xinjiang shall be a main flashpoint in the next 5–10 years when Tablighi Jamat will start implementing its final phase of Islamization of China. The region's most radical group, the East Turkistan Islamic Movement (ETIM), not only has ties to Tablighi Jamat, but is also providing the government in Beijing with a pretext for solidifying their control over the province's Uighur population. We should not forget that Tablighi Jamat is the mother of Al-Qaeda.

Of China's 1.3 billion people, about 20 million live in Xinjiang province. The region's expanding importance to China's economy, the Islamic presence in the region, and the threat of separatist and terrorist organizations under the sponsorship of Tablighi Jamat and Inter-Services Intelligence (ISI) should open eyes of Beijing to conclude that the country's northwestern frontier must not be ignored. Pakistan's brutal military dictatorship should not be trusted under any circumstances.

Islamists in Xinjiang province maintain extensive ties to Tablighi Jamat which is the religious cult and responsible for the formation of Islamic terrorist organizations including al-Qaeda, Sipah-e-Sahaba and Lashkar-e-Jhangvi. The leading terrorist organization, the East Turkestan Islamic Movement (ETIM), maintains communications with jihadist groups in Pakistan and Afghanistan. Some of its more experienced members fought with the mujahadeen against the Soviets in Afghanistan, and safe houses and cells have been uncovered everywhere from Germany to Pakistan.

In fact, certain Chinese diplomats once in Pakistan had complained to the Ministry of Foreign Affairs of Pakistan that they had information that members of ETIM were making plans to kidnap them. This plan must be sponsored by ISI since ISI is fully active in such activities. Not only do Xinjiang Islamists operate in a diverse variety of states, but foreign extremists have sought refuge in the radical sectors of China's Uighur community as well. Chinese authorities have captured Taliban militants (trained by Tablighi Jamat) in Xinjiang, and there have been reports that the Islamic Movement of Uzbekistan maintains a cell in the province. It is also worth noting that outside terrorist groups come to Xinjiang not because of a perceived regional lawlessness, but because they expect to find elements in the Muslim community that would harbor them in the name of preaching of Islam.

So, if Pakistan is left untouched despite knowing the evil designs of ISI and Tablighi Jamat, this will be a mistake. We must address the issue of disintegration of Pakistan in order to destroy the vicious and criminal organizations like ISI and Tablighi Jamat.

WHO IS GENERAL PERVEZ MUSHARRAF?

In my opinion General Pervez Musharraf is a TERRORIST-IN-UNIFORM. It is better not to judge the reality of General Pervez Musharraf by his recent actions of cooperation with USA in the so-called War-on-Terror. General Musharraf has many faces like his ancestors which make him more vicious, criminal and disgusting. Although, he never wanted to rule Pakistan, as he claimed earlier when he came from back door by removing the then Prime Minister of Pakistan Nawaz Sharif (who was an illegitimate political child of late General Zia-ul-Haq), General Pervez Musharraf began his romance with Pakistan's top political parties from Punjab in order to implement ISI's agenda of destroying USA, UK, India and Israel being a task given by the Holy Book.

Reference Pakistan's 1999's proxy invasion of Indian territory in the Kargil sector of Jammu & Kashmir, it is proven that Gen. Pervez Musharraf had long-standing links with several Islamic fundamentalist groups. Gen. Musharraf's past background has not received, from Indian and Western analysts, the attention it deserves, if one has to have a clearer understanding of his role in the proxy invasion. General Musharraf is a trained terrorist and a devoted Wahabi soldier who believes in destruction of USA, UK, Israel and India. General Musharraf is a Fascist military ruler with no conscience or sympathetic sentiments for those who have not embraced Islam. He believes in domination of Islam all over the world through holy war (Jihad) in the light of several verses of Quran as interpreted by Tablighi Jamat.

Gen. Musharraf, a Mohajir (migrant) of Azamgarh/Karachi origin, had subsequently settled down in Gujranwala in Punjab and prefers to project himself more as a Punjabi than as a Mohajir (migrant). He was commissioned in the Pakistan Army Artillery in 1964. He had an undistinguished career till the 1980s, when he caught the eye of Gen.Zia-ul-Haq and Gen. Mirza Aslam Beg, another COAS. Gen. Zia, who preferred devoutly Muslim officers in important positions, chose Gen. Musharraf for advancement as he was, like Gen. Zia himself, a devout Wahabi and was strongly recommended by the Jamaat-e-Islami and Tablighi Jamat.

The first assignment given by Zia to him was the training of the mercenaries recruited by various Islamic extremist groups for fighting against the Soviet troops in Afghanistan. It was during those days that Gen. Musharaff came into contact with Osama bin Laden, then a reputed civil engineer of Saudi Arabia, who had been recruited by the USA's Central Intelligence Agency (CIA) and brought to Pakistan for constructing bunkers for the Afghan Mujahideen in difficult terrain. Osama bin Laden initially made his reputation in Afghanistan not as a mujahideen or terrorist, but as a civil engineer who could construct bunkers in any terrain. He also developed the technique of constructing long tunnels to isolated Soviet and Afghan military posts. The Mujahideen used to suddenly emerge from these tunnels and surprise the Soviet and Afghan troops. The links, which Gen. Musharraf developed with bin Laden in those days, have subsequently remained strong.

Gen. Musharraf also developed a nexus with the narcotics smugglers of the North-West Frontier Province (NWFP). The Narcotics Control officials of the US have deliberately ignored the involvement of Gen. Musharraf in smuggling of millions of dollars of narcotics to USA and Europe because so far General Musgarraf has bought his freedom from these charges by associating and partnering with USA on War-on-Terror. General Musharraf's contacts with the narcotics smugglers are still alive and very effective while Americans have hidden this fact from being surfaced for reasons best known to President Bush. This is one of the reasons why of all the senior Pakistani Army officers of today, Gen. Musharraf has had the least interactions with the US military establishment in the form of nomination for higher training in the US, participation in seminars and exercises and visits to US military establishments. His bio-data issued by the Pakistan Army HQ. in October last at the time of his appointment as the COAS show that he has done two training courses in the UK. There was no mention of any course in the US. Perhaps this was because of his religious extremism which the then military officials wanted to hide from USA.

Gen. Zia chose Gen. Musharraf (then a Brigadier) in 1987 to command a newly-raised Special Services Group (SSG) base at Khapalu in the Siachen area. To please Gen. Zia, Gen. Musharraf with his SSG commandos launched an attack on an Indian post at Bilfond La in September, 1987, and was beaten back.

Despite this, he continued to enjoy the confidence of Zia. Gen. Musharraf has since then spent seven years in two tenures with the SSG and prides himself on being an SSG commando and projects himself as the greatest expert of the Pakistan Army in mountain warfare. When he received Gen. Anthony Zinni, the Commanding Officer of the US Central Command few years ago, he was dressed as an SSG Commando.

In May,1988, the Shias, who are in a majority in Gilgit, rose in revolt against the Sunni-dominated administration. Zia put an SSG group commanded by Gen. Musharraf in charge of suppressing the revolt. Gen. Musharraf transported a large number of Wahabi Pakhtoon tribesmen from the NWFP and Afghanistan, commanded by Osama bin Laden, to Gilgit to teach the Shias a lesson. These tribesmen under Osama bin Laden massacred hundreds of Shias. If I declare General Musharraf as a Fascist ruler functioning on the same pattern of Abu Bakr, Omar bin Khattab and Mawiya, I am not wrong.

In its issue of May,1990, "Herald", the monthly journal of the "Dawn" group of publications of Karachi, wrote as follows: "In May,1988, low-intensity political rivalry and sectarian tension ignited into full-scale carnage as thousands of armed tribesmen from outside Gilgit district invaded Gilgit along the Karakoram Highway. Nobody stopped them. They destroyed crops and houses, lynched and burnt people to death in the villages around Gilgit town. The number of dead and injured was put in the hundreds. But numbers alone tell nothing of the savagery of the invading hordes and the chilling impact it has left on these peaceful valleys." See? This is the brutal face of General Musharraf who has again struck by murdering Akbar Bugti, famous Baluch freedom fighter and a devoted soldier of Baluch nation, on August 26, 2006.

Gen. Musharraf had started a policy of bringing in Punjabis and Wahabi Pakhtoons from outside and settling them down in Gilgit and Baltistan in order to reduce the Kashmiri Shias to a minority in their traditional land and this is continuing till today. The "Friday Times" of October 15–21, 1992, quoted Mr. Muhammad Yahya Shah, a local Shia leader, as saying: "We were ruled by the Whites during the British days. We are now being ruled by the Browns from the plains. The rapid settling-in of Punjabis and Pakhtoons from outside, particularly the trading classes, has created a sense of acute insecurity among the local Shias." This is exactly what General Musharraf has done. His fascism is exposed by his acts of dishonour. General Zia became the first victim of the carnage unleashed by Gen. Musharraf on the Shias of Gilgit. Though the Pakistani authorities have not released the report of the committee, which enquired into the crash of Zia's plane in August,1988, I firmly believe that a Shia airman from Gilgit, wanting to take revenge for the May1988 carnage was responsible for the crash. Former Prime Minister of India Mrs. Indira Gandhi was also assasinated by a Sikh Security Guard who also wanted to take revenge. Such attitudes are very natural indeed. Similarly, the reason why Altaf Hussain (of Muttahida Qaumi Movement) does not come back to Karachi although his political party MQM is one of the coalition partners of the ruling Muslim League at both federal level and provincial level, it is because of this reason that there are thousands of MQM workers who want to kill Altaf Hussian because Altaf Hussain betrayed them firstly by marrying a Sindhi woman and secondly by becoming partner of army in forming government in Pakistan. They view Altaf Hussain as a traitor who sold the blood of young men from Karachi during early 90s.

Coming back to General Musharraf, during his days with the SSG in the Siachen area and in the Northern Areas (Gilgit and Baltistan), Gen. Musharraf developed a close personal friendship with the following most brutal-minded, fascist Pakistanis who can be well-termed as followers of Mawiya and Yazeed (who were the killers of children of Muhammad SA):

1. Lt.Gen. Javed Nasir, Director-General of the Inter-Services Intelligence (ISI), during Mr.Nawaz Sharif's first tenure as the Prime Minister and then served as his Adviser on intelligence matters

2. Maj.Gen. Zaheer-ul-Islam Abbasi, then a Brigadier

3. Lt.Gen. Mohd.Aziz, former No. 2 in the ISI till recently

4. Mr.Mohd Rafique Tarar, then a Judge (later became President of Pakistan during Nawaz Sharif's government).

All the above four were devout WAHABIs with strong links with Islamic fundamentalist groups like Tablighi Jamat and particularly with the Harkat-ul-Mujahideen (HUM, also known for some years as the Harkat-ul-Ansar) which was declared by the US as an international terrorist organisation in 1997. Along with the Lashkar-e-Taiba, the HUM is a member of Osama bin Laden's International Islamic Front for Jihad against the US and Israel. Lt.Gen. Javed Nasir was also an office-bearer of the Tablighi Jamaat, even while in service which clearly confirms and certifies the fact that Tablighi Jamat does play an important role in the terrorist activities in South Asia. Those who believe Tablighi Jamat to be a mere preaching group should refine their approach immediately. I have spent time with Tablighi Jamat and therefore can surely say that Tablighi Jamat is now an organ of Inter-Services Intelligence. I urge USA, UK, Australia, Philippines, Malaysia, Indonesia, Jordan and India to immediately BAN Tablighi Jamat in their countries and declare Tablighi Jamat as a terrorist organization in the disguise of relgious preaching.

In the late 1980s, Brig. Abbasi was posted as the Military Attache in the Pakistani High Commission in New Delhi. He was expelled by the Government of India in 1989 after he was caught by the New Delhi police while receiving classified papers from a Government employee.

On his return to Pakistan, Brig. Abbasi was posted to the Siachen. Like Gen. Musharraf, he had a reputation of taking rash and irresponsible actions without the clearance of his superiors. He launched an attack on an Indian army post, which was repulsed with heavy Pakistani casualties.

The late Gen.Asif Nawaz Janjua, the then COAS, recalled him to Rawalpindi and wanted to dismiss him for launching the attack without his orders, but Lt.Gen. Nasir saved him from any punishment because of the fact that Brig. Abbasi was a devout Wahabi (a sect of Islam created and propagated by Saudi Kingdom) and supporter of Tablighi Jamat's philosophy of destroying USA, UK, Israel and India.

On September 8,1995, the Pakistani Customs stopped a car carrying heavy arms and ammunition near Kohat in the NWFP and arrested its driver and Saifullah Akhtar, the then patron of the HUM. On interrogation, they reportedly told the Customs authorities that the weapons had been procured by Brig. Mustansar Billa of the Pakistan Army at Darra Adamkhel for supply to the Kashmiri extremist groups. The Pakistani army then took over the investigation and arrested a group of 40 army officers and 10 civilians headed by Maj.Gen.Abbasi. Mrs. Benazir Bhutto, then Prime Minister, alleged that this group had conspired to kill her and senior military officers, stage a coup and proclaim an Islamic state.

They were secretly tried by a military court and sentenced to various terms of imprisonment. In my opinion, the plotters had actually wanted to instal Gen. Musharraf as the head of the Islamic State, and that Gen. Aziz was also involved in the plot, but no action was taken against them for want of adequate evidence. The plotters had close links with the Hizbul Mujahideen and the Harkat-ul-

Ansar, which are known for their involvement in international terrorism. The arrested officers wanted Pakistan to become militarily involved in the Kashmir freedom struggle and make Pakistan an extremist Islamic state. "The Nation" of November 15,1995, reported: "Almost all the arrested officers are followers of the Tablighi Jamaat based in Raiwind."

Maj.Gen.Abbasi had close contacts with the Harkat-ul-Ansar. Two of the arrested officers belonged to the ISI and one of them had worked as the staff officer to Lt.Gen. Nasir, when he was DG, ISI. All these facts lead to the conclusion that General Pervez Musharraf cannot be ignored and it is not established that General Musharraf was innocent or did not know about the situation of failed coup. It is already established that General Musharraf is very close to the international terrorist groups currently operating from Pakistani soil.

Pakistani analysts were surprised when Mr.Sharif appointed Gen.Musharraf as the COAS on October 8,1998, superseding Lt.Gen. Ali Kuli Khan, a Pakhtoon, who was the CGS, and Lt. Gen. Khalid Nawaz, a Punjabi, who was the Quarter-Master General. Mr.Sharif's choice of Gen. Musharraf was attributed to the following:

* He was strongly recommended by President Tarar and Lt.Gen. Nasir (both being heavy weight champions of Wahabi Islam in Pakistan);

* He had ingratiated himself with Mr.Sharif by keeping the latter informed of the criticism of the Government's functioning by Lt.Gen. Ali Kuli Khan and Lt.Gen. Khalid Nawaz at theCorps Commanders' conferences when Gen. Jehangir Karamat was the COAS;

* Though a Mohajir (migrant), Gen. Musharraf disliked Altaf Hussain and his Muttahida Qaumi Movement (MQM). Mr. Sharif, therefore, wanted to use him to crush the MQM in Karachi.

Mr.Sharif and Gen. Musharraf got along very well till March 1999. As desired by Mr.Sharif, the new COAS set up special military courts in Karachi to try the MQM cadres on charges of terrorism. Several of them were sentenced to death and two executed before the Pakistan Supreme Court, acting on a petition, declared these courts unconstitutional. It was alleged that Mr.Sharif was also planning to have Mr.Asif Zirdari, the husband of Mrs. Bhutto, tried as a terrorist by the military courts and sentenced to death for allegedly killing Murtaza Bhutto, her brother, in September, 1996. Mr. Sharif also made the Pakistan

Army in charge of the Water and Power Development Authority (WAPDA) to bribe Pakistan Army to win their confidence.

After the visit of Mr.Strobe Talbott, US Deputy Secretary of State, to Pakistan that time, Mr.Sharif also approved a plan submitted by Gen. Musharraf for shifting Osama bin Laden's terrorist brigade from the Jalalabad area of Afghanistan to the Kargil area of India by taking advantage of the absence of the Indian army from this area during winter. While Lt.Gen. Javed Nasir strongly backed the plan, Lt.Gen, Ziauddin, the then Director-General of the ISI, expressed strong reservations over it and pointed out that it could create problems for Pakistan with the US. Gen. Musharraf transferred Lt.Gen. Aziz from the ISI to the Army HQ. as his CGS and made him responsible for its implementation through the Directorate of Military Intelligence. Lt.Gen. Javed Nasir was kept in the picture about the implementation but not Lt.Gen.Ziauddin.

While outwardly supporting the Lahore Declaration, Gen. Musharraf, with the backing of Lt.Gen. Javed Nasir, went ahead implementing the plan. Osama bin Laden's terrorist brigade was transported to Skardu in the Northern Areas and from there infiltrated into the Kargil area along with a large number of Pakistani army regulars. Mr.Sharif was allegedly not kept in the picture about sending the army regulars into Indian territory along with the terrorist brigade.

These irrational religious elements in the Pakistan army headed by Gen. Musharraf and senior retired officers who have been supporting Gen. Musharraf have embarked on this adventure in the Kargil area (India) on the basis of the following assumptions:

* The morale in the Indian armed forces is low due to the "bad leadership" of Mr.George Fernandes, then Defence Minister.

* The BJP being a party of paper tigers, known more for their "verbosity" than for their actions.

* Pakistan's nuclear and missile capability has ensured that India would not retaliate against Pakistan for occupying the ridges in the Kargil area.

* The fear of the possible use of nuclear weapons would bring in Western intervention, thereby internationalising the Kashmir issue.

* Pakistan should agree to a ceasefire only if it was allowed to remain in occupation of the Indian territory. There should be no question of the restoration of the status quo ante.

The interviews and speeches of Gen. Musharraf since October, 1998, show his thinking to be as follows:

* The acquisition of Kashmir by Pakistan can wait. What is more important is to keep the Indian army bleeding in Kashmir just as the Afghan Mujahideen kept the Soviet troops bleeding in Afghanistan.

* Even if the Kashmir issue is resolved, there cannot be normal relations between India and Pakistan because Pakistan, by frustrating India's ambition of emerging as a major Asian power on par with China and Japan, would continue to be a thorn on India's flesh. And, so long as it does so, Pakistan would continue to enjoy the backing of China and Japan.

From March 1999, Gen. Musharraf, to the surprise of Mr.Sharif, started coming out in his true colours. He issued an order that the army, as the supervisory authority, would conduct all future negotiations with the independent power producers, thereby denying any role in the matter to the politicians and civilian bureaucrats. When Mr.Sharif objected to this order, he declined to cancel it.

The COAS made out a list of all payment defaulters of the WAPDA and leaked to the press that Mrs.Abida Hussain, a Shia Minister of Mr.Sharif's Cabinet, was one of the major defaulters, thereby forcing her to resign. He has also been hinting to the press that the business enterprises of Mr.Sharif's family top the list of defaulters.

General Musharraf then insisted that he should be given concurrent charge of the post of the Chairman of the Joint Chiefs of Staff Committee, even though it was the turn of Admiral Fasih Bokhari, the Chief of the Naval staff, to hold this charge. His argument was that since the army was the most important component of the armed forces, the Chairman should always be from the army. While not accepting this argument, Mr.Sharif gave him concurrent charge for one year only, as against the normal three years. He also got himself nominated as the Strategic Commander of Pakistan's nuclear force.

By May 1999, Gen. Musharraf found to his surprise that the BJP-led Government was reacting vigorously to the invasion and had ordered the Indian Air

Force to go into action against the invaders. It was only then that he reportedly told a shocked Mr.Sharif that he had sent in a large number of Pakistan army regulars with Osama bin Laden's terrorist brigade and that the regulars were likely to incur heavy casualties. The demand of the US and other Western powers for the withdrawal of the invaders and for the restoration of the status quo ante came as another surprise to him. Despite this, he seemed to be insisting that Pakistan should not agree to any unconditional withdrawal.

Such a person like General Pervez Musharraf is a great danger to the entire humanity. If I may say, Hitler's spirit has possessed body of General Pervez Musharraf while the extreme anti-West teachings of Tablighi Jamat under the sponsorship of Wahabi Kingdom of Saudi Arabia have made General Musharraf a more brutal 'Fascist-cum-terrorist-in-uniform'. General Pervez Musharraf needs exorcism to be conducted by someone who understands the necessity of disintegration of Pakistan because Pakistan's disintegration shall pave way to destroy General Pervez and his evil military network from spreading the poison of international terrorism from Pakistan's soil.

DOCTRINE OF NECESSITY

Chapter 1 of the Charter of the United Nations dated June 26, 1945 (Article No. 1) says as follows:

'To maintain international peace and security, and to that end: to take effective collective measures for the prevention and removal of threats to the peace, and for the suppression of acts of aggression or other breaches of the peace, and to bring about by peaceful means, and in conformity with the principles of justice and international law, adjustment or settlement of international disputes or situations which might lead to a breach of the peace'

In the above chapter, it is categorically stated that UN shall take effective collective measures for the prevention and removal of threats to the peace and for the suppression of acts of aggression or other breaches of peace (which should also include terrorism being one of the breaches of peace). Hence, in view of this particular mutual understanding among all the member states, it has become necessary to address the issue in its true perspective.

Further, Articles 43, 44 and 45 of the Charter of the United Nations say as follows:

Article 43

1. *All Members of the United Nations, in order to contribute to the maintenance of international peace and security, undertake to make available to the Security Council, on its and in accordance with a special agreement or agreements, armed forces, assistance, and facilities, including rights of passage, necessary for the purpose of maintaining international peace and security.*

2. *Such agreement or agreements shall govern the numbers and types of forces, their degree of readiness and general location, and the nature of the facilities and assistance to be provided.*

3. *The agreement or agreements shall be negotiated as soon as possible on the initiative of the Security Council. They shall be concluded between the Security Council and Members or between the Security Council and groups of Members and shall be subject to ratification by the signatory states in accordance with their respective constitutional processes.*

Article 44

When Security Council has decided to use force it shall, before calling upon a Member not represented on it to provide armed forces in fulfilment of the obligations assumed under Article 43, invite that Member, if the Member so desires, to participate in the decisions of the Security Council concerning the employment of contingents of that Member's armed forces.

Article 45

In order to enable the Nations to take urgent military measures, Members shall hold immediately available national airforce contingents for combined international enforcement action. The strength and degree of readiness of these contingents and plans for their combined action shall be determined, within the limits laid down in the special agreement or agreements referred to in Article 43, by the Security Council with the assistance of the Military Committee.

The Article 43 clearly explains that all member states shall provide assistance in terms of armed forces and other facilities in order to maintain international peace. Similarly, Article 44 allows UN to use force for facilitation of peace in the world. Article 45 allows member states to assist UN in the matter of taking urgent military measures in order to maintain and restore international peace.

If we impartially evaluate the significance of the Articles 1, 43, 44 and 45, we shall establish that UN has powers to protect the whole world from aggression and terrorism. If such aggression or terrorism is committed by a particular group, UN can act to destroy such group in order to maintain international peace. Similarly, if a member state itself is involved in the acts of aggression or terrorism, the United Nations can also act to prevent the whole world from such aggression and terrorism.

In view of the fact that the socalled Islamic Republic of Pakistan has consistently committed breach of world peace by producing international terrorists and facilitating terrorism in the disguise of holy war against Christians, Jews, Hindus and other nations of the world, it has become inevitable and essential that the United Nations should take notice of such acts of Islamic Republic of Pakistan immediately. It is, therefore, necessary to invoke Doctrine of Necessity to disintegrate Pakistan in at least 5 parts in order to crush, dismantle, destroy and disrupt terrorist networks based on the soil of Islamic Republic of Pakistan.

In my humble opinion, the United Nations should urgently take into consideration possibility of disintegration of Pakistan. Following proposed UN Resolution be taken into consideration by UN Secretary General Mr. Kofi Annan:

PROPOSED UNITED NATIONS SECURITY COUNCIL's RESOLUTION ON INVOKING THE DOCTRINE OF NECESSITY IN THE MATTER OF DISINTEGRATION OF PAKISTAN

WHEREAS, Islamic Republic of Pakistan had come into existence on August 14, 1947; and

WHEREAS, questions have arisen regarding Islamic Republic of Pakistan's direct involvement in masterminding, sponsoring, promoting, facilitating, expanding, supporting, financing, helping, assisting, coordinating, cooperating, safe-guarding and organizing International Terrorist Network on its soil; and

WHEREAS, United Nations finds that there is a need to prevent the whole world from the destructive motives of Terrorists being trained, financed, promoted, supported, helped, safe-guarded and protected in Islamic Republic of Pakistan; and

WHEREAS, the opinion set forth that, when it is necessary for United Nations to invoke the Doctrine of Necessity, the United Nations should inform all member states that it is doing so, the reason that such action is necessary in the interest of the whole world; and

WHEREAS, the opinion further provided that if the United Nations must invoke the Doctrine of Necessity not just to vote, but also to form a negotiations committee to serve as a committee, then the United Nations must determine whether to act as a committee of the whole or to choose a smaller negotiations committee from among its member states after stating publicly its reason for doing so as set forth above; and

WHEREAS, in keeping with the Legislative purpose as set forth in United Nations Charter (Article No.1), the United Nations views disintegration of Islamic Republic of Pakistan in 5 parts (PUNJABISTAN, PAKHTOONISTAN, BALUCHISTAN, JINNAHPUR and SINDHUDESH) to be paramount when it is necessary to invoke the Doctrine of Necessity;

NOW THEREFORE BE IT RESOLVED that the United Nations hereby requires
to invoke the Doctrine of Necessity to adopt a resolution setting forth that they are invoking the Doctrine, the reason for doing so and the specific nature of the need to do so; and

BE IT FURTHER RESOLVED that the United Nations invoke the Doctrine of Necessity to disintegrate Islamic Republic of Pakistan in 5 parts (PUNJABISTAN, PAKHTOONISTAN, BALUCHISTAN, JINNAHPUR and SINDHUDESH) in order to destroy terrorist networks which have been nourished within the geographical limits of Islamic Republic of Pakistan;

BE IT FURTHER RESOLVED that the United Nations shall distribute this Resolution to the member states for their deliberations.

In order to understand Doctrine of Necessity, I suggest that we should take into consideration philosophy of Abraham Lincoln. As written by ALLEN C. GUELZO:

"Abraham Lincoln was a fatalist. That, at least, was what he told many people over the course of his life. "I have all my life been a fatalist," Lincoln informed his Illinois congressional ally, Isaac Arnold. "Mr. Lincoln was a fatalist," remembered Henry Clay Whitney, one of his Springfield law clerks, "he believed…that the universe is governed by one uniform, unbroken, primordial law." His Springfield law partner William Henry Herndon, likewise, affirmed that Lincoln "believed in predestination, foreordination, that all things were fixed, doomed one way or the other, from which there was no appeal." Even Mary Todd Lincoln acknowledged that her husband had been guided by the conviction that "what is to be will be, and no cares of ours can arrest nor reverse the decree." What this meant in practical terms, as Herndon discovered, was that Lincoln believed that "there was no freedom of the will," that "men had no free choice":

At other place, ALLEN C. GUELZO writes:

"Herndon is the most important source for analyzing Lincoln's fatalism, and much of the significance that this idea held for Lincoln can be seen just by how often Herndon referred back to his discussions with Lincoln about it in the years Lincoln and Herndon shared their Springfield law office. According to Herndon, Lincoln "was a fatalist and believed that fatalism ruled the world." What Lincoln meant by this, Herndon explained, was that "the great leading law of human nature is motive." All human action, in other words, begins with a reason for that action; These reasons for action are what Lincoln called "motives," and he was very clear that motives did more than simply provide the occasion for action. "Motives moved the man to every voluntary act of his life," Lincoln told Herndon. "His idea," recalled Herndon, "was that all human actions were caused by motives, and at the bottom of these motives was self."

He writes further:

"Similarly, Lincoln found no evidence in human behavior that the process of choosing or willing could be broken down into stages that might soften or divert the attractive power of motives. He maintained that there was no conscious act of any man that was not moved by a motive, first, last, and always," Herndon wrote. Thus, "there was no freedom of the will," and "men are made by conditions that surround them, that have somewhat existed for a hundred thousand years or more."

"Certainly, one has to say that Lincoln, although he won his fame and fortune as the protector of railroad property for the Illinois Central in the 1850s, also gave a utilitarian twist to the ultimate purpose of property jurisprudence. "The democracy of today hold[s] the liberty of one man to be absolutely nothing, when in conflict with another man's right of property," wrote Lincoln in 1859, "Republicans, on the contrary, are for both the man and the dollar; but in cases of conflict, the man before the dollar." Even if Benthamite utilitarianism gets no explicit credit from Lincoln in his arguments with "one, two or three" about fatalism, we cannot dismiss lightly the striking similarity of vocabulary and meaning on free will between the Springfield lawyer and the London jurist."

"Lincoln's patience sprang from his philosophy," Herndon explained, "his charity for men and his want of malice for them everywhere, all grew out of his peculiar philosophy." Since Lincoln was a "thorough fatalist" and "believed that what was to be would be, and no prayers of ours could arrest or reverse the decree," then "men were but simple tools of fate, of conditions, and of laws," and no one "was responsible for what he was, thought, or did, because he was a child of conditions."

"Not for Lincoln would there be the straightforward acceptance of a world of new horizons but rather a complex struggle to assimilate the expansion of what could be accomplished with the diminution of what one could be responsible for. His antislavery convictions may have less to do with embracing the new consciousness of the market than with an ambivalent effort to contain it. He did not live to see how futile that effort would have been in the Gilded Age, but perhaps that would not, in the end, have greatly shocked a "fatalist" like Lincoln. Why should the spirit of mortal be proud, Lincoln asked, in reciting his favorite poem, and why should it expect to accomplish more than the purposes of the Almighty had laid down for it? Perhaps that realization, more than any other single factor, left him no other explanation for human action but the "Doctrine of Necessity."

In the light of above quotations, I would like the readers to see that a great man like Abraham Lincoln was a fatalist and believer of doctrine of necessity. His concepts were based on 'hope to all'. Hence, if today, the world needs to address any particular issue like terrorism, it is essential to believe that men are made by conditions that surround them. Therefore, in order to protect mankind from any disaster, it is equally essential to invoke doctrine of necessity to repair the damage caused to mankind by acts of injustice and cruelty by any specific group or country. In the words of Abraham Lincoln:

"If we were situated as they are, we should act and feel as they do; and if they were situated as we are, they should act and feel as we do; and we never ought to lose sight of this fact in discussing the subject."

The above statement again gives a clear message that men are made by conditions that surround them.

The global conditions at present times advocate the need of invoking Doctrine of Necessity to disintegrate Pakistan in order to prevent the world from any possible terrorism which may be worse than 9/11 and more destructive in nature.

PAKISTAN IS A THREAT TO ECONOMIC DEVELOPMENT IN INDIA AND IRAN

In recent years, India and Iran have shown tremendous economic growth. Similarly, economic cooperation between India and Iran is a great symbol of Asian economic prosperity. Recently, India and Iran agreed to speed up economic cooperation amid a raging debate on Tehran's nuclear programme and the looming threat of UN sanctions. Indian Prime Minister Manmohan Singh called Iran's president Mahmoud Ahmadinejad and both expressed "satisfaction at the current state of bilateral relations," during their 15 minute telephonic conversation. They "agreed that a strong and vibrant India-Iran relationship is of strategic importance for both countries and would be beneficial for peace and prosperity of the entire region." Singh and Ahmedinejad agreed on "the need to accelerate the implementation of all ongoing cooperation projects including those in the energy and transport infrastructure sectors". The conversation was followed by a visit by Iran's Deputy Foreign Minister Mehdi Safari's to New Delhi on August 29, 2006 soon after assassination of Nawab Akbar Bugti (Baloch freedom fighter in Pakistan). India had emphasised the importance of Iran honouring the 22-billion dollar Liquified Natural Gas deal which contemplates that India would get five million tonnes of gas annually over a 25-year period from 2009. New Delhi and Tehran have also "reaffirmed their commitment" to another multi-billion dollar gas pipeline that will transport gas from Iran's southern Pars field to India via Pakistan.

It is to be noted that India has categorically opposed the use of force to compel Iran to give up its nuclear plans though New Delhi has twice voted against Tehran at the International Atomic Energy Agency, criticising its atomic programme. Tehran says the programme is for generating electricity and has sought talks on Western concerns though it ruled out a formal moratorium on enrichment.

On the Iranian economic front, a German trade official belonging to the German-Iranian Chamber of Industry and Commerce (DIHK), Michael Tockuss recently declared that Iran is a major economic power in the Middle East. In his words: "It (Iran) is the only country in the region which has a serious industry production and has a mid-and long-term potential to develop and expand these economic cores". Similarly, Tockuss also predicted a further increase in German exports to Iran. German exports to Iran stood at around 3.8 bln euros in 2005. Iran remained Germany's top trading partner in the Middle East last year with a total trade volume of 4.3 bln euros, surpassing the United Arab Emirates and Saudi Arabia.

In view of recent economic development plans and mutual cooperation between Iran and India, Pakistan's role is obviously very suspicious for the following reasons:

1. Being a safe haven for terrorists, Pakistan's military dictatorship and Inter-Services Intelligence (ISI) may decide to disrupt economic cooperation between India and Iran by creating border conflicts;

2. Pakistan's ISI being involved in spying for USA against Iran on issues concerning Uranium enrichment, may decide to mastermind any potential attack on Iranian nuclear research centres in connivance with the terrorist groups based in Afghanistan;

3. Baluchistan being a province seeking independence from Pakistan has already become a bone of contention between Iran and Pakistan;

4. Pakistan being a Wahabi state would never like to see a prosperous Shia Iran on relgious grounds of jealousy and hatred;

5. Pakistan being a political prostitute dancing on the music of its foreign masters, may decide to crush Shia community living in Pakistan through a sectarian violence sponsored by ISI and Pakistan Army-backed religious factions;

6. Pakistan being a model of military dictatorship fascinated by Islamic Fascism of Wahabi model, may be used by Saudi Arabia to destroy Iran with a motive to decrease influence of Shia Islam in the region;

7.   Pakistan's involvement in international drug trade on a very large scale may affect the relationship between Pakistan and Iran;

8.   Pakistan may kill Shia religious scholars based in Pakistan to spark sectarian clashes in Pakistan in order to find excuse to cleanse Shia communities in different parts of Pakistan including Waziristan;

It is, therefore, very important on the part of both India and Iran to closely see the attitude of Pakistan towards their economic development and mutual cooperation in economic sectors. Pakistan's brutal military dictatorship assisted by its cruel agency called Inter-Services Intelligence (ISI) may cause severe troubles to India and Iran at any moment. Hence, disintegration of Pakistan is as crucial as Global Warming. We must cut the wings of Terrorism which are nourished on the soil of Pakistan.

PROPOSED NEW STATES IN SOUTH ASIA

In order to address the issue of terrorism in a way to clearly reflect what should be done by the United Nations and world powers in true perspective, it is important that the South Asian geography be completely changed whereby Pakistan be disintegrated into 5 parts.

Following new states should come into existence under the supervision of the United Nations through a unanimous UN Resolution as discussed in another chapter of this book:

1. BALUCHISTAN

2. SINDHUDESH

3. PAKHTOONISTAN

4. JINNAHPUR

5. BALAWARISTAN

6. PUNJABISTAN (being the remaining part of Pakistan which may still call itself 'Pakistan')

BALUCHISTAN

One of these new states shall be BALUCHISTAN. Southern Pakistan's Baluchistan region is one of the most rugged and remote lands in the world. Pakhtoonistan and Baluchistan have long complicated Afghanistan's relations with Pakistan. Controversies involving these areas date back to the establishment of the Durand Line in 1893 dividing Pashtun and Baluch tribes living in Afghanistan from those living in what later became Pakistan. Afghanistan vigorously protested the inclusion of Pashtun and Baluch areas within Pakistan without providing the inhabitants with an opportunity for self-determination (Plebiscite).

Since 1947, this problem has led to incidents along the border, with extensive disruption of normal trade patterns. The most serious crisis lasted from September 1961 to June 1963, when diplomatic, trade, transit, and consular relations between the countries were suspended.

Divided in the nineteenth century among Iran, Afghanistan, and British India, the Baloch found their aspirations and traditional nomadic life frustrated by the presence of national boundaries and the extension of central administration over their lands.

A long-dormant crisis erupted in Balochistan in 1973 into an insurgency that became increasingly bitter in recent years. The insurgency was put down by the brutal Punjabi Army in the name of National Security, which employed criminal methods and sophisticated equipment, including American helicopter gunships, provided by USA and flown by Punjabi pilots. The deep-seated Baloch nationalism based on tribal identity had international as well as domestic aspects. As the insurgency wore on, the influence of a relatively small but disciplined liberation front has increased so much so that Baluchistan is now ready for its independence.

Former Prime Minister of Pakistan Bhutto (who was judicially murdered by General Zia-ul-Haq) was able to mobilize domestic support for his drive against the Baloch in order to keep them under the umbrella of Pakistan. Punjab's support was most tangibly represented in the use of the army to put down the insurgency. One of the main Baloch grievances was the influx of Punjabi settlers, miners, and traders into their resource-rich but less populated lands. External assistance to Bhutto was generously given by the then Shah of Iran, who feared a spread of the insurrection among the Iranian Baloch. Some foreign governments feared that an independent or autonomous Balochistan might allow the Soviet Union to develop and use the port at Gwadar, and no outside power was willing to assist the Baloch openly or to sponsor the cause of Baloch autonomy.

By early 1974, an armed revolt was underway in Baluchistan, the southwestern region of Pakistan bordering on Afghanistan and Iran. In northwest Pakistan, populated mainly by ethnic Afghan-Pashtuns, insurrectionist sabotage was a common occurrence. The extent of the Daoud regime's involvement in these insurrections has been a matter of some debate, but he clearly was allowing Baluch resistance fighters to set up bases in Afghanistan, and was providing sanctuary to Pashtun dissidents who were under warrant of arrest in Pakistan.

To retaliate against Afghanistan's actions, Pakistan provided funds, material and weapons to Islamic fundamentalist organizations and other anti-Daoud Afghan extremists conducting raids and sabotage inside Afghanistan. These operations were not intended to overthrow Daoud but to force him to negotiate. This could explain why Iran, at the same time it was offering economic aid to Daoud and pressing him to resolve the conflict with Pakistan, was also supplying US weapons and equipment to the insurgent groups in Afghanistan. Some of this material went through Pakistani channels and some passed directly to groups operating in western Afghanistan. Iran, because of its own sizable Baluch community, had its own motives for seeing the armed revolt in Baluchistan quelled, and provided Pakistan with US helicopters for use in this effort.

During the mid-1970s, Afghanistan was preoccupied with its own internal problems and seemingly anxious to normalize relations with Pakistan. India was fearful of further balkanization of the subcontinent after Bangladesh, and the Soviet Union did not wish to jeopardize the leverage it was gaining with Pakistan. However, during the Bhutto regime hostilities in Balochistan were protracted. The succeeding Zia ul-Haq government took a more moderate approach, relying more on economic development to placate the Baloch.

Following the Soviet invasion of Afghanistan, there were about 600,000 Afghan refugees in Pakistan by the summer 1980; 500,000 (largely Pushtuns) in the Northwest Frontier Province and another 100,000 in Baluchistan. By late 1980 the number was closer to one million.

The province of Baluchistan, which borders both Iran and Afghanistan, is being used by Inter-Services Intelligence (ISI) and Pakistan Army for cross-border smuggling and has more recently been infiltrated by former members of the Taliban and Al Qaida operatives who are functioning close cooperation and liaison with ISI. Armed battles between clans are frequent. Because the provincial police presence is deliberately kept limited by General Musharraf, travelers wishing to visit the interior of Baluchistan should consult with the province's Home Secretary. Advance permission from provincial authorities is required for travel into some areas. Local authorities have detained travelers who lack permission.

Quetta, the provincial capital, has experienced serious ethnic violence that has led to gun battles in the streets and the imposition of curfews. The recent murder of Nawab Akbar Bugti who was the freedom fighter of Baluchistan has finally proved that Pakistan Army and ISI would do anything in order to keep their existence untouched by forces which may cause disturbance to an integrated Pakistan. The North West Frontier and Baluchistan remain feudal holdouts. General Pervez Musharraf has had to undertake delicate balancing to carry out operations against Baluch freedom fighters in these areas. There has been talk of rising secessionist feelings in Baluchistan.

By 2004 Baluchistan was up in arms against the federal government, with the Baluchistan Liberation Army, Baluchistan Liberation Front, and People's Liberation Army conducting operations. Rocket attacks and bomb blasts have been a regular feature in the provincial capital, particularly its cantonment areas, Kohlu and Sui town, since 2000, and had claimed over 25 lives by mid-2004.

The Gwadar Port project employed close to 500 Chinese nationals by 2004. On 03 May 2004, the BLA killed three Chinese engineers working on the Port. Gwadar airport was attacked by rockets at midnight on 21 May 2004. On 09 October 2004, two Chinese engineers were kidnapped in South Waziristan in the northwest of Pakistan, one of whom was killed later on October 14 in a botched rescue operation. Pakistan's military government blamed Iran for fanning insurgency in Baluchistan in order to please USA.

The Baluchistan case now rests upon the more exalted principle of self-determination. Pakistan is the champion of self-determination but its own people do not enjoy any democratic rights. The three pillars upon which the Pakistani State rests are Allah, Army and America. The people of Pakistan do not figure in this scheme at all. The Pakistani leaders want a diplomatic engagement with India on Jammu and Kashmir. Pakistan's socalled prime minister Shaukat Aziz has once again donned the cloak of democracy that hangs outside General Pervez Musharraf's bunker.

Baluchistan is a mountainous desert area of about 3.5 lakh sq kms and has a population of over 7.5 million or about as much as Jammu and Kashmir's population. It borders Iran, Afghanistan and its southern boundary is the Arabian Sea with the strategically important port of Gwadar on the Makran coast commanding approach to the Straits of Hormuz. Quetta is the capital of Baluchistan. The population consists mainly of Baluch and Pathans. Like the Kurds, the Baluch are also a people ignored by the makers of modern political geography. There is an Iranian province of Sistan and Baluchestan spread over an area of 1.82 lakh sq kms and with a population of over 2.5 million. Its capital is Zahedan.

Through most of their history the Baluch administered themselves as a loose tribal confederacy. The Baluch are an ancient people. In 325 BC, after his abortive India campaign, as Alexander made his way back to Babylon through the Makran desert, the Greeks suffered greatly at the hands of marauding Baluchis. The legend has it that they originally came from near Aleppo in Syria and there is much linguistic evidence to suggest that they belong to the same Indo-European sub-group as the Persians and Kurds. They came into Islam under the shadow of the sword of Mohammad bin Qasim's conquering Arab army in 711 AD.

Whatever be their origins, by 1000 AD they were well settled in their present homeland. The poet Firdausi records them in the Persian epic, the *Book of Kings*, thus: *'Heroic Baluches and Kuches we saw/Like battling rams all determined on war.'* As relatively late arrivals in the region, the Baluchis had to battle earlier occupants of the lands such as the Brahui tribes who still abound around Kalat. The Brahui language belongs to the Dravidian family of languages and is close to Tamil. Quite clearly, the Brahuis are the only Dravidian survivors in northern India, after the Aryan invasion.

A restless people, the Baluchis naturally pushed eastwards towards the more fertile regions watered by the Indus river, but were halted by the might of the Mughals. But we still have reminders of the many Baluchi incursions in the names of towns like Dera Ghazi Khan and Dera Ismail Khan in the Punjab and NWFP. Unlike the Dravidians of Mohenjodaro and Harappa who disappeared without a trace, the Brahuis made one last hurrah when they asserted their power in Kalat.

By the 18th century Kalat was the dominant power in Baluchistan and the Khan of Kalat was the ruler of the entire region. But the Brahuis paid for it by getting assimilated into the majority Baluchis. The Brahui language still survives in small pockets but only by just. My late father who served in British India's Defence Services Staff College at Quetta in the early 1940s would often tell me of hearing local tribesmen serving in the Staff College speaking a language that sounded remarkably like Tamil!

The British first came to the region in 1839 on their way to Kabul when they sought safe passage. In 1841 they entered into a treaty with Kalat. In the wake of Lord Auckland's disastrous invasion of Afghanistan, the British annexed Sind in a mood, Mountstuart Elphinstone said, was that 'of a bully who had been kicked in the streets and then goes home to beat the wife in revenge!' The British annexed Sind in 1843 from the Talpur Mirs, a Baluchi dynasty.

On June 27, 1839 Ranjit Singh died and within 10 years his great prophecy on being shown a map with British possessions in India in *ek din sab laal ho jayega!* came to be true. After the formal surrender of the Sikhs on March 29, 1849 and the annexation of Punjab, the British now had a long border with the Baluchis. But learning from their disastrous experience with the Afghans they preferred to keep out of harm's way on Baluchi assurances of the inviolability of their borders.

In 1876, the British however forced another treaty on the Baluchis and forced the Khan of Kalat to lease salubrious Quetta to them. The Khan's writ still ran over Baluchistan, but now under the watchful but benign eye of a British minister. That the Khan of Kalat was not considered another insignificant prince was in the fact that he was accorded a 19-gun salute. With security assured and largely unfettered domestic power the Khan led lavish and often eccentric lifestyles. One Khan collected shoes, and to ensure the safety of his collection had all the left shoes locked in a deep dungeon of his fort in Kalat!

Whatever the whimsicalities of the Khans of Kalat, like the rulers of Hyderabad and Kashmir, they enjoyed the greatest degree of autonomy possible under the system established by the British as long as whimsy was within reason and not inimical to British interests. This arrangement prevailed till 1947. The urge to be independent rulers burned equally bright in all three of them. The Khan of Kalat, Mir Ahmad Yar Khan, went further than Hari Singh of Kashmir and Osman Ali Khan of Hyderabad. He declared independence, while the other two dithered and allowed events to overtake them. Unlike in Hyderabad, it was apparent that the population largely supported the Khan.

The Baluchis, like the Pathans of NWFP, were not too enthused with the idea of Pakistan. In the NWFP the separatist Muslim League led by Mohammed Ali Jinnah was actually rejected in elections. Yet eight months after the Khan's assertion of independence the Pakistanis forcibly annexed Baluchistan. But Baluchi aspirations for an independent state were not quelled completely. In 1973 a war of independence broke out in Baluchistan. For five long years there was total war.

At its peak the Baluchis raised a force of 55,000 combatants. Nearly six Pakistan Army divisions were deployed to fight them. The Pakistan Air Force was also deployed and its Mirage and Sabre fighter jets carried out strikes all over rural Baluchistan. Widespread use of napalm has been documented by scholars like Robert Wirsing of the University of Texas and Selig Harrison. Iran too joined in the military action and Huey Cobra helicopter gunships of its Army Aviation were widely used. By the time the last pitched battle was fought in 1978 5,000 Baluchi fighters and 3,000 Pakistani soldiers had died. Civilian casualties were many times that. The Baluchi war for independence was crushed, but the aspirations still flicker.

Speaking at the 57th session of the Commission of Human Rights at Geneva between March 9 and April 27, 2001, Mehran Baluch, a prominent Baluch leader said: 'Our tragedy began in 1947, immediately after the creation of Pakistan. The colonialist army of Pakistani Punjab forcibly occupied Kalat at gunpoint.' Even now a struggle continues in Baluchistan. Leading Baluchi leaders like Sardar Attaullah Mengal, Sardar Mahmood Khan Achakzai and Nawab Khair Baksh Marri, heads of the three great Baluch clans, have been leading protests over the economic exploitation of the region's great natural resources to the exclusion of the local people. Marri and hundreds of his supporters are under arrest.

Till 1977 the Indira Gandhi government actively worked for the democratic aspirations of the Baluchis and Pathans. Baluchi fighters were trained in the deserts of Rajasthan. India also provided them with financial and diplomatic assistance. With Bangladesh free, Indira Gandhi reckoned that Sind, Baluchistan and Pakhtunistan should follow.

After her electoral defeat in 1977, Vajpayee as the Janata government's foreign minister made his first misguided and woolly-headed attempt to normalize relations with Pakistan. Indian support to various movements struggling for self-determination in Punjabi-dominated Pakistan was withdrawn. L K Advani was as much a comrade in arms then as he is now for he did not protest even when G M Syed's Jiye Sind movement was betrayed. He was quite pleased with being able to go to his hometown of Karachi and visit his old school.

Vajpayee's assurances to Zia, the man who initiated the policy of 'death by a thousand cuts' to destroy India, ensured that the Baluchis were forced to leave their camps in Rajasthan and all financial, military and diplomatic assistance was cut. Even though the Janata Party regime did not last very long, the damage was done.

However, Independent Blauchistan shall definitely crush the terrorist network spread by Pakistan Army and Inter-Services Intelligence (ISI) on its soil. An Independent Baluchistan shall ensure that unlawful military camps of Pakistan Army which are engaged in training future terrorists on its territory shall be destroyed.

SINDHUDESH

More than 20 million people living in Sindh (excluding Karachi), the southeastern province of Pakistan that was once home to the ancient Indus Valley Civilization, have been engaged in non-violent resistance to the fundamentalist ideology of Pakistan for the last fifty years. Some months back, Congressional Human Rights Caucus held hearings on the human rights situation in Pakistan. Congressman Tom Tancredo observed:

"The treatment received by the Sindh province in Pakistan is also of concern. Sindhis are peace loving, nonviolent Sufis, supportive of the American values of democracy and secularism, and opposed to terrorism and nuclear arms. However, they continue to be marginalized by the Pakistan government, and are negatively affected by the Pakistani government's efforts to dam the Indus River."

Vibrant Sindhi communities numbering in the tens of thousands exist throughout the world. These Sindhis condemn the terrorism and Talibanization of Pakistan and advocate democracy and civil society for all the nationalities. In January 2005, Governor Rick Perry of Texas said in a message to Sindhi-Americans:

"Sindhi-Americans continue to play an important role in promoting peace, democracy, and human rights. By putting thought into action, you have reinforced the importance of being civic-minded, committed citizens, and I wish you continued success."

Pakistan is currently under the control of a military government that denies the peoples of its smaller provinces, especially Sindh, Balochistan and NWFP (Pakhtoonistan) their due political, economic, social, and cultural rights. Over the last few years, the Pakistani military government has received several billions of dollars in international aid from the USA, EU, Japan, and other donor countries under the pretext of its role in the "war against terrorism." In reality, the current military dictatorship continues to promote Islamic fundamentalists, impose medieval laws against women and minorities, and teach religious intolerance and anti-Semitism in schools. Pakistan's role in nuclear proliferation severely threatens the peace and security of the region.

Existence of Sindhudesh shall not only seek to compensate these injustices and attrocities but also to provide an insight into the peace loving, pacifist and liberal minded culture of the Sindhis to move on the road of prosperity through a new country called SINDHUDESH.

The concept of Sindhudesh is not very new. Sindhudesh was also a dream of late Ghulam Murtaza Shah Syed (generally known as G.M. Syed) son of Syed Mohammed Shah Kazmi, descendant of a famous saint of Sindh. He was born at the village Sann in Dadu District, Sindh, on January 17,1904. His father passed away when he was only sixteen months old. He has had no formal schooling. Whatever he learnt, was self-tutored. By dint of hard work, he attained mastery over Sindhi and English languages. He was also conversant with Arabic and Persian languages. History, Philosophy and Political science were his favorite subjects of study. At an early age of fourteen years, he started his career as an activist. In 1919 he became Chairman of School Board of his own town.

Subsequently, he was elected as a President of Karachi District Local Board in 1929. He later became its President. In 1930, he organized Sindh Hari (peasants) Conference and became its Secretary. In 1937, he was for the first time elected a member of Sindh Legislative Assembly.

In 1938, he joined the All-India Muslim League. In 1940, he became Minister of Education in Sindh. In 1941, he became one of the members of the Central Committee of the Muslim League. In 1943, he became President of Sindh Muslim League. In 1944, he played a pivotal role in politics and got a resolution passed in the Sindh Assembly in favor of Pakistan, which was the pioneer resolution of its kind in the whole of undivided India. In 1946, conditions compelled him to dissociate from the Muslim League, and formed a new party named Progressive Muslim League. The same year he was elected as leader of the Coalition Party in the Sindh Assembly. In 1954, he acted as Chairman of Sindhi Adabi Board. In 1955, he played an active part in the formation of Pakistan National Party. In 1966, he founded Bazm-e-Soofia-e Sindh. In 1969, he formed Sindh United Front. Getting disappointed from All-Pakistan national politics, he founded in 1973 the 'Jeay Sindh' (Freedom Movement of Sindh) movement. Mr. Syed was the author of more than sixty five (65) books. His books are on numerous subjects, ranging from literature to politics, religion and culture etc. He was himself a mystic had a lot of love and regard for mystics of all faiths. Besides being a man of immense learning, Mr. Syed possessed a personality that was graceful and poised. Highly cultured and refined manners, hospitality and geniality were the two glaring traits of his character. Wit and humor were the keynotes of his personality. He respected all genuine difference of opinions. For decades, Sindh and Sindhi people had constituted the center of his interest and activity, and all his love energies were devoted to their good. GM Syed proposed the Pakistan Resolution, 1940 in the Sindh Assembly, which ultimately resulted in the creation of Pakistan. However, he became the first political prisoner of Pakistan because of his differences with the Brutal Punjabi military leadership of Pakistan which was quite inevitable since Punjab's military dictatorship never wanted any genuine politician to survive on the soil of Pakistan. G.M. Syed had firmly believed that criminally motivated Punjabi military dictatorship had deceived the Sindhis.

In 1971, disappointed with the national politics, GM Syed found no option but to demand the Right of Self Determination for the people of Sindh. Mr. G.M. Syed is founder of 'JEAY SINDH' (Freedom Movement of Sindhis) Movement which is aimed at achieving SINDHUDESH. For his bold expression of opinion and views after the creation o Pakistan, he was been kept either in jail-or in solitary confinement for the: period of more than 30 years.

On 19th January 1992, GM Syed was put under house arrest and his house was declared a sub-jail. He was detained without trial until his death. G.M. Syed is declared **"Prisoner of Conscience"** by Amnesty International.

Sindhudesh shall be a country filled with love and equality for Muslims, Hindus, Christians and Buddhists living on its soil. Sindhudesh shall never allow any continuation of illegal terrorist activities which are currently done by Pakistan Army and ISI on its soil in order to disrupt Indian peace.

PAKHTOONISTAN

The North West Frontier Province (NWFP) of Pakistan borders with Afghanistan. Pakistan Army and Inter-Services Intelligence (ISI) have been very active in exploitation of this province for terrorist activities in the region and for training of future terrorists in camps situated in different parts of NWFP. The people living in NWFP are called 'Pathans'. The Pathans live in NWFP and Afghanistan. The group is made up of some 60 Pushto-speaking tribes. The Pathans or Pakhtoons number some 10 million in Pakistan and some 8 million in Afghanistan. They make up the largest ethnocultural group in Afghanistan.

The Pakhtoons comprise of various groups. Some live as nomads in the high mountains with herds of goats and camels; others, such as those living in the Swat Valley, are farmers; and still others are traders or seasonal laborers. However, this ethnographic description defies the fact that they constitute more than 20% of Pakistan's armed forces and dominate Pakistan's transportation industry and have provided the most popular Pakistani president Ayub Khan who lead the major industrialization movement which Pakistan has seen in the last 59 years.

The British attacked the Pathans in the late 19th and early 20th century. They were finally forced to offer the Pakhtoons a semiautonomous area between the border of British India and Afghanistan. After the creation of Pakistan in 1947, the new nation annexed the Pakhtoon border regions. In the early 1950s, the Soviet Union through Afghanistan supported Pakhtoon ambitions for the creation of an independent Pakhtoonistan in the border areas of West Pakistan. Several border clashes and ruptures of diplomatic relations between Afghanistan and Pakistan ensued. Pakhtoons also helped liberate the part of Kashmir which is now under Pakistan's control. Their support and hospitality to more than four million Afghan refugees was crucial in Afghan's liberation from the Soviet Union.

The Pakhtoons are known as people who are brave, simple, and sincere in their dealings with others. They are noted as fierce fighters, and throughout history they have offered strong resistance to invaders. They staunchly hold on to their cultural traditions and connect with one another in a visceral way. Most are guided by a tribal code of ethics, Pakhtunwali, or "way of the Pakhtun (Pathan)." Tribal customs and traditions make up the biggest part of the Pakhtoon society. The tenets of Pakhtunwali show the true essence of Pakhtoon culture and these rules are followed religiously. It incorporates the following major practices: hospitality and protection to every guest; the right of a fugitive to seek a place of refuge, and acceptance of his bona fide offer of peace; the right of blood feuds or revenge; bravery; steadfastness and righteousness; persistence; defense of property and honor; and defense of one's women.

An independent Pakhtoonistan will become hurdle for the terrorist activities being sponsored and controlled by Pakistan Army and Inter-Services Intelligence in association of Tablighi Jamat which is the most popular religious group in this region. Tablighi Jamat has been very effective in mobilizing Pakhtoon volunteers to fight in the name of Islam (holy war known as Jihad) through their lectures and religious cultism in order to prepare an army of ignorant fighters who do not possess any knowledge about their own religion except reading 5 prayers in a day.

The new Pakhtoonistan will be an independent country with its own power to make decisions in order to build a country free from terrorism and its sponsors. Independent Pakhtoonistan will delink Pakistan Army and ISI with the terrorist camps being nourished by Pakistan Army and ISI on the soil of Afghanistan being an attempt to Talibanize the region. Similarly, a new Pakhtoonistan will secure the newest Afghan democracy from any possible brutality by Pakistan Army and ISI.

Pakhtoonistan was also dream of great Asian freedom fighter Khan Abdul Ghaffar Khan (known as Bacha Khan). His efforts to see his people as a free nation could not be transformed into reality during his life time but now his dream will certainly be turned into reality in the form of Pakhtoonistan.

In my opinion, Bacha Khan was a great leader from Asia apart from Gandhi of India and Dr. G.M. Syed of Sindh. I have written a specific petition in which I have appealed to the Norwegian Nobel Committee to award Nobel Peace Prize to Bacha Khan. Following is the extract of my petition:

To: Norwegian Nobel Committee
Give Nobel Peace Prize to Bacha Khan
A Pakhtoon Nelson Mandela born in Asia

This Petition is specifically addressed to The Norwegian Nobel Committee, Henrik Ibsens gate 51 NO-0255 Oslo, Norway and for special consideration by former Nobel Peace Prize laureates, Members of National Assemblies of Pakistan and India, leaders of peace research institutes & institutes of foreign affairs and former Advisers at the Norwegian Nobel Institute. The purpose of this petition is to highlight the greatness and competence of a great peace-maker called KHAN ABDUL GHAFFAR KHAN (commonly known as BACHA KHAN) who devoted his entire life for preaching peace and welfare of people.

Bacha Khan was a freedom fighter for his people against the vicious British Empire in India. There is no denial to the fact that the life story of Bacha Khan is in itself the history of Pakhtoons full of patience and self-determination, life-long trials and tribulation, courage and grim resolve which sprang from a consciousness of virtue, unpretentious life-style and his unbeaten struggle to liberate his people from the domination of the British Empire. Bacha Khan was a man of commitment who firmly believed that liberty is Almighty God's gift to mankind. Hence, in his opinion, the obligation to respect liberty of mankind is equally sacred. It goes without saying that Bacha Khan, the great Pakhtoon hero of courage ruled over the hearts of his people, who with a voice that did not err, lived for the sake of serving the sadly neglected Pakhtoons. He was and still is the eternal symbol of Pakhtoon's pride and courage. Bacha Khan waged a relentless non-violent struggle against the British colonial rule which was full of exploitation, hatred and conspiracies. Bacha Khan was an Asian NELSON MANDELA of his time who always remained sincere, steadfast in his actions, served no personal ends, gained no titles and was indeed a man of great character.

Bacha Khan suffered the tortures of solitary confinement, heavy chains on his hands and feet, dirt and filth and lice and hunger, and most of all insults and kicks from the lowest and most inferior British soldiers. He was always a model prisoner like Nelson Mandela. He was a kind man and gentle even with his enemies. He forgave every thing to everyone, and possessed unlimited patience. He treated his captors with sublime contempt.

Bach Khan's ordinary attitude and behaviour portrayed his moral personality. With a mind free of fear and prejudice, honouring him as a legendary politician of the Indo-Pak subcontinent, Bacha Khan himself was greater than the legend. He was looked upon, respected and adored as a saint politician by his millions of followers. He was, no doubt, not less than a real saint to rise against the mightiest power on earth with his invincible determination and unshakable resolve launching a formidable non-violent struggle against the then British rulers. Bacha Khan stood for, fought for and suffered for his people exactly in the same manner like Nelson Mandela of South Africa. This very fact lent support to his will and determination in learning to survive despite obstacles and hardships that rendered strength and elevation to the freedom struggle. Once a close companion of Bacha Khan complained bitterly about the inhuman and ruthless manner in which the Red-Shirt volunteers were made a target of torture by the British Colonial Administration, Bacha Khan consoled his companion and told him not to lose faith, rather set about doing good to people. This was exactly what Nelson Mandela did in South Africa.

Bacha Khan was always subjected to trials and political persecution. Being a great humanist, he ardently believed that human nature was not so worthless as to hinder it from respecting goodness in others. It is easy to look down on others but to make an estimate of our failing is difficult. God's blessings, according to Bacha Khan, are marked for those, who submit to God's will and serve Almighty God through selfless activities for the overall good of humanity at large irrespective of caste, colour, race or religions. To Bacha Khan's mind, love was useful to further strengthened his character. Deeply influenced, it pro-

duced in him a holiness that fortified his faith and convictions, elevating the spirit of those whom he served selflessly.

Bacha Khan is no longer with his people. His love, affection, lifelong sufferings in the service of Pakhtoons and safeguarding the spirit of Pakhtoon traditions will remain a great source of inspiration. The great and the finest Pakhtoon freedom fighter Khan Abdul Ghaffar Khan (Bacha Khan) did not fail since he lived and died for a great and noble cause. The sweet remembrance of the legendary Bacha Khan shall flourish everlastingly while he sleeps peacefully in his lightning grave.

I, therefore, urge The Norwegian Nobel Committee Henrik Ibsens gate 51 NO-0255 OSLO Norway, former Nobel Peace Prize laureates, Members of National Assemblies of Pakistan and India, leaders of peace research institutes & institutes of foreign affairs and former Advisers at the Norwegian Nobel Institute to nominate BACHA KHAN for Nobel Peace Prize of 2007. I want all peace-loving people of this world, who believe in fight for freedom and struggle for elevation of mankind, to sign this Petition. This will prove that our world is still a place of good human beings who can recognize and salute good men.

SYED JAMALUDDIN
FRANCE
TEL +33 679113805
FAX +1 775 269 9669

Source:http://www.PetitionOnline.com/SyedJam8/petition.html

JINNAHPUR

Jinnahpur, as its name suggests, shall represent followers of Muhammad Ali Jinnah who was a secular-minded leader of the then India. Muhammad Ali Jinnah had vision of a country where people should remain free from any dictatorship (military or otherwise) and live in a conducive political environment.

However, the *Pakistan* formed by Muhammad Ali Jinnah and his supportive freedom fighters turned out to be a deadly and ugly experiment when Jinnah and his true friends soon realized and discovered that the elite of Punjab consisted of enemies were ready to stab Pakistan in its back. But, before something could be done by either Jinnah or his accomplices, Punjab implemented its vicious plans by assassinating both Muhammad Ali Jinnah (though offcially he died a natural death) and Liaquat Ali Khan who was the first Chief Executive of Pakistan. It is my firm belief that Muhammad Ali Jinnah was poisoned to death while every one knows that Liaqat Ali Khan was killed in a broad day light by a hired assasin who was engaged by the then Punjabi elite. Henceforth, there was no other hindrance in the way of Punjab to hijack the country within few years.

The only political resistance came from Fatima Jinnah, sister of Muhammad Ali Jinnah, but like always, the crazy and hypocrite religious scholars advocated against the leadership of a woman and began a campaign against her in Pakistan in order to disrupt her political plans to save Pakistan from the cruel hands of Punjab's military dictatorship. Hence, the then Army Chief Ayub Khan who was founder of Pakistan's military dictatorship and who was fully brainwashed by Punjabi religious scholars while he also enjoyed moral and financial support of Punjabi politicians, did all what was required of him to obstruct the democratic forces from seeking political power in the country. The hypocrite religous scholars of that era supported Ayub Khan simply to prevent Fatima Jinnah from becoming the Chief Executive of Pakistan.

This is very interesting that the main supporters of Ayub Khan were the WAHABI scholars (who are even today dominating the Pakistan politics through the offices of ISI) who considered themselves to be champions of Islam. Pakistan's military is todate inclined towards the same WAHABI Group represented by Tablighi Jamat and Jamat-e-Islami in Pakistan. These Wahabi scholars stood up against Fatima Jinnah during 60s. In recent years, the same hypocrite Wahabi scholars also stood up against Benazir Bhutto and issued religious decrees against her during 90s to prevent her from becoming Prime Minister of Pakistan. However, in view of the fact that these Wahabi scholars oppose the leadership of a woman on religious grounds, they do not have any answer to the historic fact about Ayesh (widow of Holy Prophet Muhammad) who had come out of her house and led her army to fight against Ali (Son-in-law of Holy Prophet Muhammad). These Wahabi scholars remain quiet and embarrassed if challenged to explain the reasons and justification of Ayesha's decision to lead her army against another Muslim. In my opinion, these Wahabi scholars purposely do not open their mouths against Ayesha because she had raged war against Ali (son-in-law of Muhammad) whom the Wahabi scholars consider as their enemy out of jealousy and hatred.

Coming back to point, Jinnahpur will be a homeland for Urdu-speaking people including Christians and Hindus living in Karachi apart from other communities. It is also suggested that about 10 Million more Christians and Hindus should migrate to Jinnahpur from India. The main political force to govern Jinnahpur shall be elected by the people of Karachi. The most prospective political force to rule Jinnahpur shall be MQM-Mutahida Qaumi Movement under the leadership of Altaf Hussain who is although currently part of the present Government in Pakistan on grounds of Doctrine of Dissimulation (taqiyyah), but firmly believes in the need and importance of a free country for Urdu-speaking people. Doctrine of Dissimulation (taqiyyah) is allowed in Islam which states as under:

It is related from Imam Sadiq in an authenticated tradition:
taqiyyah is my *din* (religion) and the *din (religion)* of my forefathers. Whosoever has no *taqiyyah* has no *din (religion)*.

It was the motto of the household of the Holy Prophet so as to protect themselves and their followers from harm and bloodshed, and to better the condition of the Muslims and to cause agreement among them, and restore them to order during the initial days of Islam. Doctrine of Dissimulation within the teachings of Shia Islam contemplates that the shia community and their Imams (Religious Leaders) have suffered much and have been denied their freedom throughout history, and that no sect or people have suffered like them, thus, they have been forced on many occasions to practice *taqiyyah* (Dissimulation) in order to conceal themselves from those with other beliefs and to keep themselves and their practices hidden, as long as their religion and their survival was threatened. Dissimulation has been commanded in the Qur'an:

« not he who is compelled while his heart is at rest on account of his faith » (16:106).

This verse was revealed about 'Ammar ibn Yasir, who took shelter by proclaiming unbelief in order to protect himself from the enemies of Islam. Another Quranic verse says: « And a believing man of pharoah's people who hid his faith...» (40:28).

Jinnahpur shall be composed of Karachi, Hyderabad and other small nearby cities. These cities have population of Urdu-speaking immigrants who had migrated from India at the time the creation of Pakistan in 1947. The main reason for a specific country called Jinnahpur is due to the fact that the grip of the landed oligarchy in the Sindh over the rural population continued to be a main cause of the growth of inequality in Pakistan for the last 59 years. MQM always wanted to rid the country of the medieval feudal system, and to rid Urdu-speaking popluation from the domination of Punjab. One important reason for the creation of Jinnahpur is also that such Urdu-speaking migrants remain marginalized, even though they were the principal speakers of Urdu, the national language of Pakistan. In response to chronic unrest in Sindh Province, in June 1992 the army was called in to assist police in restoring law and order. In November 1994, the army was withdrawn from law enforcement duties in Sindh, but the paramilitary Rangers were reinforced and specially trained police inducted. in 1995 and 1996, hundreds of people were killed by Rangers and police, including dozens of members of the Muttahida Qaumi Movement (MQM).

Going back to check recent history of Karachi which involved sectarian violence, including bombings, experienced an upsurge in 1996 throughout this port city. Although by the end of the year the government quelled much of the violence in Karachi, it never produced any political settlement that would provide a lasting peace.

The Punjabi military dictatorship attributed most terrorist acts in Karachi either to MQM, or to the Shaheed Bhutto group of the Pakistan People's Party, which was led by former Prime Minister Benazir Bhutto's brother until his death in a clash with police on 20 September 1996. The Pakistan Muslim League (PML) led government of Nawaz Sharif was elected in February 1997, and consolidated its grip on power by gaining a majority in the upper house as a result of the Senate elections in March 1997. It secured 23 of the 49 seats available in the Senate Elections, bringing the PML(N) strength in the Senate to 30 out of 87, and with the support of its allies—the Awami National Party (ANP), the Muttahidda Quami Movement and the Tehrik-e-Jafria Pakistan (TJP), it controlled a majority of 44 seats.

The ANP and the MQM subsequently departed from the coalition. Tensions in Karachi experienced a disturbing resurgence in 1998, primarily as a result of fighting between Urdu-speaking population and the provincial government. Responding to the violence, the Government of Pakistan on 28 May 1998 made a promulgation of Emergency under Article 232 of the Constitution. This was done on the recommendation of Inter-Services Intelligence (ISI) because ISI never wanted Karachi out of their control either politically or socially since the influence of MQM in Karachi was not acceptable to Punjabi military dictatorship.

That time, first part of this three-pronged strategy was to isolate Urdu-speaking population from the rest of the communities in the country, and this policy was underway through physical, psychological, social and political isolation of such

Urdu-speaking population. The Inter-Services Intelligence (ISI) forced a military operation against Urdu-speaking population in 1992 to legitimise the illegal and brutal actions against them. The Inter-Services Intelligence deliberately used the army, knowing fully well that an army is the symbol of any country's national solidarity and when the same army starts action against any particular community, the message other communities get from this is that the action is legitimate. And even if they deem the action inappropriate, they should not have the courage to speak against it because of the involvement of the armed forces. Through the policy of isolation of Urdu-speaking population, Inter-Services Intelligence (ISI) forced the MQM leadership either to go underground or seek refuge in exile.

The link between the leaders and their people was severed aiming at disintegration of the movement. Urdu-speaking people were brutally terrorised so that they quit the MQM and accept slavery. While the Urdu-speaking population in general and the MQM in particular, were victimised through ISI-sponsored false and fabricated stories about existence of "torture cells" run by MQM. MQM was accused of terrorism on the national television (PTV), in the newspapers and magazines while MQM's fabricated brutalities were publicised so much so to make people of Pakistan hating the party. This government sponsored propaganda aimed at defaming MQM as a terrorist organisation internationally.

Further during late 90s, under this policy of isolation, Inter-Services Intelligence (ISI) supplied weapons, vehicles and money to a specific militant group formed by ISI in Karachi to kill MQM workers and sympathisers and allowed them a licence to carry out broad-daylight terrorism and mass killings. The process of isolation is still on through the present State operation against Urdu-speaking population in general and the MQM in particular, because Inter-Services Intelligence (ISI) knows that unless a community is isolated from the others, any repressive action against it is not possible. That is why Urdu-speaking population and MQM were being accused of anti-State activities and tagged as Indian or RAW agents.

Inter-Services Intelligence (ISI) had initiated the propaganda all over Pakistan that only the "sons of the soil" have rights to live in Pakistan, while the Urdu-speaking population are not accepted as "sons of the soil". Urdu-speaking population have been portrayed as aliens and Inter-Services Intelligence (ISI) has created a situation in the country through its venomous propaganda, branding them as traitors.

Similarly, under severe Islamic extremism sponsored by ISI in almost all parts of Pakistan, the miseries of the Christians in Pakistan are enormous and visible everywhere and at every level. Pakistan came into being on August 14, 1947, after the partition of the sub-continent of India which was under British Rule due to the Political struggle of different political leaders. Even though the founder of the nation had said on August 11, 1947, "The religion has nothing to do with State Affairs", but now the religion of Islam has a dominating status in the Constitutionalized political, judicial, social, cultural and governmental systems. Islam is the official state religion. Being enforced as the supreme law of the Land is the Islamic Shariah, the judiciary, legislature and executive are also working under the constitutionalized law. All the laws are being modified and reframed according to the injunctions of the Quran, which is the Holy Book of Muslims.

The present constitution, political system and government are undemocratic. No more Democracy. Theocracy is prevailing in Pakistan. Under this system, the Christians of Pakistan have neither equal political, socio-economical status, nor the equal access to available opportunities in playing a leading role in the national set-up. Though Christians believe and consider themselves to be first class citizens of Pakistan, the present political system believes the Christians are second class citizens and are practically at the lowest level. The fact is, Christianity has been in existence since the first century, while the Islam and Muslim came much later in the subcontinent of India.

Constitutionally, no Christian has the entitlement to become President, Prime Minister, Chairman of the Senate, or the Speaker of National Assembly (Parliament) of Pakistan. Under the Constitutional bindings, the policies and practices have been adopted by all government and judicial functionaries to ignore and neglect the Christians every time, everywhere at all levels.

None of the Christians are in a position as the Chief of Army, Navy, Air Forces, Paramilitary forces, police, CIA (Pakistan), FIA, CID or etc. There are no Christian Commissioners, Deputy Commissioners, Assistant commissioners. There are five Sectariates (four provincial and one federal) comprising of a different departments where you cannot find in all of Pakistan. In the judiciary, there are no Christian Judges in any High Court, while there are four High Courts, Supreme Court, Federal Shariah Court, nor is there any Christian judge working as a District Session Judge in Pakistan.

Same situation prevails in Education and other departments. The doors of the jobs and entries to get education at lower and higher levels have been closed under unwritten conventions. The Christian Educational institutions, which were running and managed by the churches were taken over by force, nationalized by the Bhutto government in 1972. Now, no more Christian character is being seen in these Islamized Christian Institutions. Lots of other non-Christian Institutions have been denationalized and given to their real owners but the reason is not known why the Christian Institutions are not being denationalized and given to the churches. The present government is bent upon the policy of privatization of Public Revenue Run Sectors, but the government is very much reluctant to take any step to hand over the Church properties-institutions to the churches in Pakistan. At present, more than 5000 jobs, which were for Christians are now held by the Wahabi Muslims because of influence of ISI and its allied relgious group known as Tablighi Jamat. Because of this the 5000 or more Christians have been forced to be unemployed and thousands of dependents have been deprived of their livelihood. These institutions were the basic centers for learning, social and cultural gatherings, spiritual development for the Christians. Christian teachers, professors, or students are not seen there. Now these institutions are the dens of automatic weapons and training centers for religious terrorism.

Due to the nationalization of Christian Educational Institutions and abolishing of the reserved seats for minorities in the government institutions in 1972, there has been an increase of the Christians in illiteracy and poverty. At present, 4% of the women and 8% of the men from the Christian community are literate. Therefore 96% women and 92% men are suffering in the extreme darkness of illiteracy and poverty. According to the liberal press media in Pakistan, hundreds of Islamic religious schools, called "Madrasas" are run by different Religio-Political Parties and groups which were allowed and funded by late General Zia-ul Haq (military dictator).

These socalled 'Madrasas' are the training camps where terrorism is taught, promoted and supported on very scientific lines. It is indeed the greatest truth that the soil of Pakistan is currently used for International terrorism. Pakistan's disintegration shall pave way for a trouble-free environment for Urdu speaking people under the banner of 'Jinnahpur'. Muslims, Christians and Hindus of South Asia shall make Jinnahpur a place of moral justice and mutual love.

BALAWARISTAN

In the ancient period of human civilization the northern most part of Jammu and Kashmir was spread over Kalash Mansarowar from Ladakh side to Swaat in Dardistan side. Much of its past is known through the mythology of its people as the written history is of very recent in origin. It is believed that in the early 7th century of civilization a fierce war took place some where in present Baltistan side between the forces of China and Tibet lasting for several years. As a result of this prolonged war the region got divided into sub regions with separate rulers for each region. Historians have also named this pre disintegrated period as Greater Ladakh but the exact composition and existence of such a kingdom is found no where in history. During the days of wilderness and disintegration, people from the neighbouring countries of Tibet, Dardistan, Mongolia etc. migrated in tribes or groups and settled down in the uninhabited places of Changthang, Zanskar, Shaam, Baltistan, Purik, Dras etc. Today's population in these regions mainly consist of mixed origins of Mangols and Dard races with no ethnic divisions having similarities in language, culture, dress and food habits.

The great religions of the world, Buddhism, Islam and Christianity reached Ladakh through missionaries, carried out in most peaceful manner. Buddhism reached Tibet from Kashmir where it became the religion of the rulers and masses and influenced the rulers and masses in Ladakh. In those days Kashmir was the centre of activities for Buddhist studies and missionaries. Renowned Buddhist scholars and preachers of great fame like Rinchin Zangpoh (a Kashmiri pandit by origin) also came to Ladakh on preaching mission. Similarly Islam also reached Ladakh from Central Asia, where the rulers and masses had embraced the new religion around 9th century of the medieval period. Kashmir had become the centre of Islamic preaching through missionaries of renowned scholars and saints. Conversion from one religion to another through peaceful means and humble preaching maintained communal harmony among all communities for centuries till it was used by individuals and institutions for political and personal interest in recent times.

Partition of India in 1947 brought many changes in J&K State also. An armed conflict took place between India and Pakistan over Kashmir soon after the partition. This conflict was followed by an agreement of cease fire through a U.N resolution in 1949. Around one third of the state went under the occupation of Pakistan, which was named as Azad Kashmir but Gilgit and Baltistan were not included in Azad Kashmir, rather named as Northern Areas. The area came under the direct control of Federal Government of Pakistan (Pakistan Army) with no rights of representation either in Pakistan-occupied Kashmire Assembly or in the National Assembly of Pakistan (Parliament). Government of India, people of the areas and people of Kashmir including the leaders from Indian side of Jammu and Kashmir protested against this move.

During the last 59 years, this region also witnessed several bloody conflicts between India and Pakistan in 1948, 1965, 1971 and lastly in 1999 when the conflicts known as Kargil War attracted world attention because of the severity and sensitivity in the background of both countries possessing Nuclear capability. The highest and costliest battle field in the world is also located in this region on the glacier of Baltoru and Saltoru known as Siachen. Huge number of human lives are lost every year on both sides of these glaciers due to hostile weather conditions.

This land of Gilgit and Baltistan shall be called 'Balwaristan' which includes present districts of Diamer, Skardu, Ganchhe, Gilgit and Ghazer and Pakistan-occupied districts of Chitral and Shinaki Kohistan where there has been an undeclared ban on speech and writing since the past 59 years.

Like all colonies, this heaven on earth, which has abundant resources, is occupied by strangers (Pakistan). It is Pakistan and it's corrupt military dictatorship which has captured the great land. Neither has it bought it on lease nor has it signed any written agremeent with the people of this land. This useless and wicked Pakistan entered like a guest as a sympathiser and helper but became a host due to simplicity and foolishness of the owner of the house. By making brothers fight with one another, it made the real host a slave in his own house.

Pakistan got this occupation without any efforts or loss at the time when company commander Hassan Khan (who was retired by Pakistan as Colonel later) of 6 J & K regiment and Subedar Maj. Gilgit scouts Raja Babar Khan revolted against the ruler of Jammu & Kashmir and arrested his appointed Governor, Brigadier Ghansara singh and established an independent state of Gilgit on Ist November,1947. Baltistan was liberated by the Gilgit scout and local people in 1948. The actual reason of revolt was delay in meeting the demands of timely incentives to Gilgit scouts due to animosity of R.C Kak, the then Maharaja Hari Singh's Prime Minister, with the governor. Only 9 Platoons of Gilgit Scouts from Nagir, Hunza, Gilgit, Punial, Gopis, and yasen and a few local civilians played an active role in the revolution. After the arrest of Ghansara Singh, military revolutionary council, led by Capt. Mirza Hassan Khan, appointed Raja Shah Raees Khan as President of the Republic and Mirza Hassan Khan as Commander-in-Chief of the army. The British commandent of Gilgit scouts, Major Brawn who was opposed to the revolution and was trying to flee via Chitral was arrested.

After humiliating the heroes of the revolution, disbanding Gilgit scouts and demolishing its historical contonment, Pakistan finally gave credit of this so-called freedom to Maj. Brawn and decorated his wife with a medal after a passage of half a century.

It may be recalled that rulers of Jammu & Kashmir, while respecting the importance of this great land and the aspiration of the people, had granted it a provincial status. The Maharaja never thought that with the grant of provincial status, muslims would be benefited. There may be demerits in the setup of the Maharaja but during his period, no muslim shedded the blood of another muslim. Nor he fanned the secretarianism and prejudice like Pakistani occupants.

Pakistani usurpers, by buying a few traitors of this region, snatched away this gift of the Maharaja. They caused severe damage to the economy, politics, cultural and historical heritage and religious hormony of this region, through the Pathans, who were the worshippers of wealth, and converted this heaven like land into a decaying Pathan colony, while India is still honouring state subject rule in spite of rebellion in the Indian occupied Jammu & Kashmir. No single person has been settled by India in Jammu and Kashmir till today. Neither non-state person can acquire the citizenship there, nor purchase any property. While Pakistan is making all its efforts to settle Pathans in Pakistan occupied Kashmir (POK) but no Kahsmiri is ready to accomodate Pathans in the name of religion or sect, like in Balawaristan. As a result, Pakistani rulers and internationally notorious intelligence agency (ISI) are facing difficulties in penetrating Pathans in PoK.

United Nations Commission for India and Pakistan (UNCIP) also provides protection to the state subject rule and Pakistan had been asked that it must pull out its whole army and civilians, who are not residents of Jammu & Kashmir, including Balawaristan within three months, from January 5,1949 when the second resolution passed. Instead of complying with the UNCIP resolution, Pakistan sent armed Pathans in disguise to the disputed region, in such an organised manner, that Gilgit Baltistan even today presents the scene of a Pathan colony.

Moreover, Pakistan cheated the UN so much at the time when the U.N. observers visited occupied Gilgit Baltistan in 1949, Sardar Alam, political agent, appointed by Pakistan, was presented in the disguise of head of local authority by giving him the cover of Gilgit cap and Chogha. In the begining, Numberdars (village heads) were introduced as members of the local authority. Since 1971, the civilised world is being kept in dark by describing the so-called puppet Northern Areas council as ruling class, but Pakistan's face is about to be exposed sooner or later. Now no one will believe its lies and hypocracy.

When Pakistan was admonished at the U.N. on India's complaint several years ago, it again got Balawaristan (Gilgit Baltistan) declared a part of Jammu & Kashmir state, through wickedness and temptation and denied the freedom of this region, so that in case of a plebiscite, entire Jammu & Kashmir could became a part of Pakistan due to votes of these simple hearts and foolish Gilgiti Balties.

But the situation today is different. It must be remembered that on August 13th, 1948, UNCIP, resolution grants the right to choice one of the three options. It is the discretion of the people of Jammu & Kashmir (including Gilgit Baltistan) that they vote in favour of Pakistan or India, through right of self-determination or they vote in favour of their independent state.

The new Balawaristan shall be a country of its sons of soil while strangers and aliens (like Pakistan's military dictators) will have to leave this land.

978-0-595-41766-7
0-595-41766-3